Amma Mia!

STORIES,
ADVICE &
Recipes
FROM ONE
MOTHER
to another

Amma Mia!

Esha Deol Takhtani

FOREWORD BY JAYA BACHCHAN

EBURY
PRESS

An imprint of Penguin Random House

EBURY PRESS

USA | Canada | UK | Ireland | Australia
New Zealand | India | South Africa | China | Singapore

Ebury Press is part of the Penguin Random House group of companies
whose addresses can be found at global.penguinrandomhouse.com

Published by Penguin Random House India Pvt. Ltd
4th Floor, Capital Tower 1, MG Road,
Gurugram 122 002, Haryana, India

First published in Ebury Press by Penguin Random House India 2020

ISBN 9780143449171

Typeset in Adobe Caslon Pro by Manipal Technologies Limited, Manipal

Printed at Repro India Limited

To my Picola, my little angel up in heaven,
who first sparked my motherly instinct

Contents

Foreword

Just as a caterpillar's transformation into a butterfly is not as simple as sprouting wings and flying away, a woman's transformation into a *mother* is certainly not as simple as giving birth and returning to life as it was. Once a woman has crossed into the realm of growing new life within her, she is changed. Her life is changed, inevitably and permanently, by the metamorphosis of motherhood. Motherhood is not all cuddles and kisses. It is difficult, messy and exhausting. A mother is vulnerable and yet strong. She is 'full', loving her child so completely and she is 'empty', loving her child so completely.

'Munia', as I fondly call Esha, has evolved so gracefully from the young loving child I knew into a woman of substance—a mum to two lovely daughters.

It is not often that I open a book and find that I have much in common with the author's point of view or find the compatibility that I feel when I read the book, like I do with *Amma Mia*. Honestly, it is beyond my comprehension why Munia chose me to write the Foreword for her book, more so since I have long relinquished my role as a full-time mother and now have grown-up grandchildren! Maybe, just maybe, she identified with my experiences of evolving as a 'mother' and 'grandmother', choosing to surrender to the mystery of the needs of our children and the surprises they bring, just as we would surrender and adapt to the surprises brought by new love.

Her book *Amma Mia* shares information and advice on how to make mothering a more rewarding job while raising happier, healthier children. It's for anybody who wants to be a new mom, is a new mom, or wants really good reasons to be a new mom.

I sincerely congratulate Esha for her maturity and focus in life, for wanting nothing more than what she sees with the purity of her heart. May God bless her and her family always.

Jaya Bachchan

Introduction

'I am going to be a great mom!' say most mothers before their delivery.

And once the baby arrives into this world, when you've realized that the diapers have run out in the middle of the night, or when the breast pump won't work, or when dark circles ring your eyes because your baby won't sleep at night or when you find yourself in a room, crying for no apparent reason, it's natural to suddenly feel—even momentarily—that you may not be such a great mom after all. All of a sudden, you realize that being a scientist at a space agency would probably be easier than raising a healthy and happy baby.

But that's far from the truth.

For one, scientists probably have it harder.

Secondly, every mother is a great mom, who, with a few tools and the help she deserves, could be even better.

That's what I realized a few months after Radhya was born. All new mothers are clueless. And the fact that there is an overabundance of information today doesn't really help. In fact, it can make things more confusing. One day my life was utter chaos, and by the next it was not, because I had had an epiphany about motherhood and how we moms can help ourselves. Of course, while helping out our babies! This epiphany was the reason I wrote this book.

But why listen to *me*—a celebrity mom who probably has an arsenal of help at her disposal?

Because I'm no different from you. If there's one state of mind that erases all boundaries of class and caste, it's motherhood. In this book, I come to you not as a celebrity, but as a city mom who is tackling the challenges of being a new mother. And because, in this case, my being a celebrity has nothing to do with how good I am as a mother. They are two different jobs. My role as a celebrity is one thing, but my being a mother is just me. And how refreshing that is for a change!

My maternal instinct makes me a hands-on mom. It doesn't allow me to be anything else. I've always listened to my inner voice, and in this case, it was loud and fierce.

From the moment I knew I was pregnant, I was a 100 per cent sure that I wanted to be present for my children for every moment in their lives. I made a conscious decision to take a step back from my career, slow down and only take up projects that would allow me the freedom to do a fabulous job of raising my children. Also, I believe in living each phase of life to its fullest and giving the right people and aspects their due: whether it was my career then, or as a responsible new wife, or today as a mother. Since the age of eighteen, I've worked hard and been dedicated to the film industry. I started working in 2000 and my first two films—*Na Tum Jano Na Hum* with Hritik Roshan and *Koi Mere Dil Se Poocho* by Boneyji—were released almost simultaneously in 2001. I never had time to date, to hang out with friends or to have a thriving social life because I had focused all my energies into my career, which, as we all know, is a really demanding one—my days were spent waking up before the sun, on the job for days without a break, away from family and friends without respite till the film was complete. Most young girls at that age are going to college, dating, going to clubs and just enjoying their youth. I didn't have most of these experiences, but I made up for it by working extra hard and carving out a name for myself in the cut-throat world of films.

So when I knew I was going to be a mother, I channelled that same energy and drive into doing a damn good job of this too. The choice was mine, and I'll never have it any other way. I believe that half-baked effort is no effort at all, and so, I brought this attitude with me to invest in motherhood, and it pays off rich dividends every day when I see my baby daughters, Radhya and Miraya, happily eating from the meal plan I organized and plated or gleefully playing under my watchful eye!

Please don't get me wrong. It's not like I'm some kind of superwoman. I've made many mistakes as a new mother learning on the job, but that hasn't discouraged me from trying again and again, or being curious, or unlearning and then re-learning. As a celebrity, I could've thrown up my hands in despair when things were getting too hectic and hire a battery of help to take care of my daughters. And yes, I do have help, but it has always been my battle to fight. The mistakes I make, in fact, make me soldier on and push me to be better. I do everything myself when it comes to my babies (as you'll find out when you read this book). Like I mentioned, my being a celebrity has nothing to do with my performance as a mother. They don't mix, much like oil and water.

Of course, being in the spotlight has its ups and downs. I won't go into the negative aspects because there's no fun in cribbing. When it comes to the positive aspects, there are many. People look up to us as role models— for guidance, for tips and advice. And my fans (mothers, among them) who follow me on social media, the ones who want to know my diet or skincare regime, will perhaps be a bit disappointed when they read this book to know that there's no magic bullet to turn us into fantastic moms.

You need to put on your apron, get to work and get your hands dirty, just like everyone else. And so this is a book about me, Esha Deol Takhtani—not a celebrity but a person, flawed and full of potential. Someone who is a planner, a realist, leaning towards OCD behaviours, bursting with stories of motherhood that she'd like to pass on to all the new mothers who need some hand-holding, some friendly advice or just a laugh.

The idea for this book popped into my head one day, in the middle of a toddler-feeding crisis, which you will read about later in the book. It got me thinking about what I was doing wrong and how I could be better. And as I dug deeper, more things surfaced, things that are not necessarily discussed in everyday mom talk. These include: the guilt, questioning whether mothers deserve free time, and more seriously, post-partum depression, which I too faced briefly. I realized that I didn't know of a book that talked about all these issues, while also tackling the problem of what to feed a toddler. This, as my paediatrician, Dr Ravindra Chittal, MD, DCH, (you'll meet him again in the course of this book) says, is the number one most asked question by new mothers.

What began as madly scribbled notes on post-its and napkins, gradually began to take shape into something coherent. From then on, I have been on a creative journey— gathering recipes, tweaking old ones, creating them anew—to make my children's gastronomic experience an enriching and nutritious one. I have included all these simple, delicious and innovative recipes at the end of the book, which I hope will help you plan your babies' meals. Dr Chittal is someone I trust blindly. With his advice, combined with my husband's, my childhood experiences with food and, most importantly, my own motherly instincts (trust me, there is nothing better than a mother's instinct), I began my journey as my babies' Amma to Chef Amma Mia.

This book also features the voices of the many women I spoke to during the writing process: from doctors, paediatricians, nurses, nannies to mothers, including mine. I have gathered all their advice and tips and presented it in an easy to read manner for you.

This book is an offering, in which I share with you my stories, advice and strategies that worked for me and made my experience as a new mother simpler.

This is my baton of experience and now I'm passing it on to you.

1

Little Miss Deol and the Missing Idlis

I started out as an unfussy toddler who ate—rather drank—anything I was given. My mother, Hema Malini, remembers how anyone feeding me would switch my bottle of milk for another filled with tomato juice (my favourite, apparently) or banana juice and other concoctions, which I would happily and sleepily guzzle. Perhaps I acquired a taste for tomatoes, which is the reason why I'm a huge fan of Virgin Mary's—and other tomato-based curries—and always order one when I'm out for a meal.

Every mother hopes that their child turns out to be an unfussy eater, and so, my mother too was surprised, and pleased that I never said no to the many juices they'd hold out in front of me. But little did she know that I was soon going to turn food on its head.

As I grew up, my mealtimes came to be known as the great family tamasha. Propped up on my child seat, my mouth full of food, the entire family, sometimes the cooks themselves, would gather in front of me to put on a show for my benefit. The help would dance and the would nannies sing—to amuse me and also show off their talents in front of my mother—the occasionally passing staff would cheer me on as someone stealthily shovelled a spoon of food into my reluctant mouth. Since I was a relatively chubby kid with rather round cheeks, it was hard to tell whether I'd swallowed my spoonful. In truth, I would hoard it all in my mouth, swallowing nothing—only to spit it out on the unsuspecting victim who'd had the bad sense to stand in front of me. It was safe to say I was more than a handful when it came to food.

It is not uncommon to find children who, otherwise happy and compliant, balk and dig in their heels when it comes to eating. Food can be either a bore or a break in the usually carefree routine of a toddler. While writing this book I thought hard and long about why I was the way I was: one of the things that struck me was that food, or eating, always came with the bludgeon of threats. I know that countless mothers, house help and grandmothers have resorted to this tactic in a moment of frustration or to improve their efficiency because the good-ol' scare seems to work like magic. In this chapter, I want to examine a child's eating habits and consider what makes them tick and what doesn't, and to do so I am going to use my life as a template.

As a four-year-old, I had learnt to fear many things. Usually, they came in the form of the hapus-wallahs (alphonso sellers), who'd tread the quiet, leafy lanes of Juhu Scheme in the hot summer afternoons. Their shouts of 'Hapus-wallah! Hapus-wallah!' would pierce the afternoon stillness and puncture my cheer; for me, nothing could be worse than the peddler of mangoes. My help, who had been entrusted with feeding me, instilled the wrath of the poor mango sellers in me. '*Dekho dekho*,' they'd scare me into finishing my food, '*hapus-wallah aa gaya hai. Khana nahi khayega to hapus-wallah le jayega* [Look, look, here comes the alphonso seller. If you don't eat, he'll take you away.]' It sounds funny now but back then I used to be petrified at the mere mention of the hapus-wallah and would swiftly, albeit grudgingly, eat my food. The other constant threat used to make me and my sister, Ahana, eat was: '*Agar khana nahi khayenga toh Papa ko bolenge* [If you don't eat your food, I'll tell Papa.]' So, every time my father, Dharmendra, would come home, my sister and I would be really scared of interacting with him. It was only much later in life that I realized that my dad is not the terror they had made him out to be. He's one of the most soft-hearted, sweetest people I know. He doesn't even like to shout. But the staff at home had instilled in us a fear of him.

I grew up in a hardcore traditional south Indian household. My grandparents were Brahmin Iyengars who'd moved to Bombay in 1965. Our home was always bustling with women, and my grandmother, Jaya Chakraverty, was the chief matriarch. She was a very strong woman and an extremely talented artist, painter, producer and writer. In fact, she rewrote the Mahabharata and the Ramayana in Tamil and produced many films. She's the rock who made my mother who she is today. My grandmother's sisters—Shanta aunty and Saroja *mami*—also followed her to Bombay. So we were a large household, filled with Shantaji's kids, Prabha and Mohan—my aunt and uncle; my cousins from Bombay, who would stop by daily and the ones from Chennai, who would visit us often. And the thronging traffic at home was primarily composed of strong, independent women.

In a traditional setting like ours, it is obvious that our food too was classical south Indian fare, which was made especially by two excellent Brahmin cooks— Rukmani mami and Govindachari—who had come from Chennai to live with us and manage the pantry and kitchen. We followed some strict culinary rules— no non-vegetarian food, no eggs, even mushrooms were considered non-veg. My grandmother, along with her two sisters, would oversee all the kitchen operations. And it was a massive operation.

Everything we ate was made from scratch. Every day, rice flour and dosa atta were prepared, spices and chutneys were ground on massive granite *sil-batta*s, *dose kals* and large vats of curd were set. Attached to the kitchen was a huge storeroom with floor-to-ceiling steel containers holding all our ration—dals, different varieties of rice, flour and spices. I was fascinated by this room and would often sneak into it and open the smaller *dabba*s for a peek. Sometimes, when my friends and I would play house, I would collect spices and other condiments from here to fill my little *katori*s and take them to my room. If the cooks found me here, I'd be reprimanded. They were always telling me to not touch the things in there and I guess that made me want to do it all the more. Food was always served on banana leaves and all of us sat down on the massive ten-seater dining table and ate together. Our home had the reputation of serving the best south Indian food in the city. Everyone who dropped by was offered an authentic cup of filter coffee, made by Shanta aunty, a brilliant cook who accompanied my mother on all her shoots.

But you know what they say about too much of a good thing . . . Our family was very particular about eating but they weren't necessarily gourmands. This meant that we ate pretty much the same thing every day. Simple, basic, traditional south Indian food. Idlis, sambhar, coconut chutney, curd, dal, roti, sabzi, tomato and lemon rice, rasam and, of course, dosas—but not masala dosas because my grandmother didn't consider them authentic. There was nothing fancy, nothing out of the box about our food. No pastas, no pizzas, nothing. Although the food at home was fantastic, as a child I soon grew bored of it.

Every morning, my younger sister, Ahana, and I ate breakfast, our backs against a massive window, under the watchful eye of my grandmother who sat in front of us. Before she ate, my grandmother would toss a few bits of idli out of the window for the crows. It was her ritual, a tribute paid to our ancestors. It was a kind thought, even though we spent most of our time together giggling and ducking from the idli line of fire. The menu was fixed: it was idli every day and we had had our fill; and as children, we found creative solutions to break this unrelenting monotony. So while one of us would distract my grandmother, the other, within this two-second respite, would swiftly take the idlis, place them under the plate and squash them flat. Since there were no idlis on our plate, we'd be allowed to head to school. Only much later would they unearth our uneaten idlis, but by then we would already be at school—Jamnabai Narsee—heartily digging into our delicious two-rupee vada pavs.

As a child, food wasn't important to me. I wasn't intrigued by food and I definitely wasn't a foodie. Food was yet another chore in our daily routine: get up, brush your teeth, drink your milk, have your breakfast, idli, dosa, sambhar. Repeat. Even at school, my lunch dabba came from home and it was quite boring. However, that being said, things began to change gradually.

One day, when I was in the second standard, a new girl joined our class. Our first term had already started, and she had joined the class a little late. She was quite a chubby kid so initially, not too many people wanted to be friends with her. When she came and sat next to me in class, I, too, tried to play it cool and remained aloof. But during lunch time, she opened her tiffin box and sweetly offered me the *nashta* that her mother had packed. Without knowing what it was, I took a bite and found that I really liked it, so I asked her what it was. To my horror, she told me that it was French toast and that it contained eggs. I was terrified. I'd eaten 'egg'! It was totally forbidden at home. I thought I'd done something terribly wrong. Later, when my mother found out about my transgression, she wasn't angry at me. Instead, she managed to get the cooks to sneakily make French toast for me. It was my first brush with egg and I loved it. I am forever thankful to Payal Lohia, the girl who opened up this world to me. She is still one of my best friends today. We call the episode our very own French Toast Connection.

There were still more surprises awaiting me.

My father, a *pukka* Punjabi, would often take us to Lonavala on the weekends for a quick family getaway. We would always stay at Fariaz Hotel. My father would book an extra room adjacent to ours where he would host a few friends with whom he'd play cards and hang out. There was one thing I'd always wondered about: my father, who otherwise did everything with us, usually took his meals separately. Once, I happened to slip into the other room and discovered a big, covered dish. My sister and I were curious about what lay hidden under the cover, so we opened it and were shocked to find the remains of a monstrous insect. I examined the remains of the insect and asked my help, Bharti, '*Ye kya hai? Itna bada keeda kidhar se aaya hai?* [What's this? Where did such a big insect come from?]' Bharti said, '*Ye keeda nahi hai, ye lobster hai.* [This isn't an insect. It's a lobster.]' To which I replied, '*Ye kaun khata hai ye sab?* (Who eats this stuff?)' She giggled and said, '*Papa ne khaya hai!* (Your father ate it!)'

That's when I realized that my father was not like us. He is not a vegetarian; in fact, he's just the opposite: my dad is a hardcore non-vegetarian. But in front of my mother, he only eats vegetarian fare, perhaps because he's respectful, or because he's scared of her. That was the first time I saw a lobster thermidor, albeit completely cleaned out.

The monotonous food at home meant that we were always tempted to eat out. We would look forward to being invited to our friends, Luv and Kush's (Shatrughan Sinha's kids) home or to Sonam and Ria Kapoor's home because it was only in their houses that my sister and I got to eat anda curry. Obviously, my mother knew what we were up to, and she encouraged us because egg, rich in protein, is healthy for a growing child's diet.

The other temptation was the delicious tiffins that my friends brought to school. My dear friend, Amruda Nair, currently the owner of Leela Hotels, would bring delicious fare from the hotel and we would attack her dabba during lunch break. In fact, Amruda's dabba was the reason we also got bullied. During the break, we'd all sit in a circle on the floor of the basketball or throwball court. One of my friends, Sikandar Kher, who is now in the film industry, used to be really big and fat back then. On Thursdays, Amruda's dabba consisted of butter chicken from the Leela, and Sikandar would find us and come and sit squarely on our backs, jumping on us, demanding her dabba. He wouldn't leave till we had handed it over to him! Of course, I couldn't understand what the fuss was all about because, being a vegetarian, I had never even tasted it.

Often, looking at all the yummy food our friends would bring, things their mothers had cooked up in a storm, Ahana and I would feel sad. Back home, we'd ask our mother why she never cooked for us like all the other mothers. My mother had never entered the kitchen; she didn't have the time for it. Many years later, she told me that my grandmother had banned her from entering the kitchen. She had told my mother, '*Naan vone kala kahe pethir key* [I've given birth to you for the *kala*, art, not the kitchen.]' Of course, I don't blame my mother for anything because she's dedicated her life to films and dance, and is a successful woman in her sphere of work. But it's not like she never tried her hand at cooking either.

During our summer vacations, we'd rent an apartment in London for a month. It was always a fun time because we would all be together, trying our hand at normal housework—like washing the dishes or going to the laundromat. It was during these holidays that my mother actually started to cook a little and we relished the food she made. Everyone who has stayed outside their country for a while suffers from food-homesickness at some point. My mother would make us rasam and rice, and another dish, which she had learnt from her colleague and friend, Dimple aunty (Kapadia). It was a hit with us. The recipe was simple—torn up bits of pav and paneer, curry leaves, haldi and salt, all sautéed in a *tadka* with ghee—but boy, did we devour it! It was during our travels that I actually tried different kinds of food; I discovered that I enjoyed the taste of Thai cuisine and loved fondue. These moments were refreshing culinary distractions from the food we ate at home.

As I grew up and shed my baby fat, I was drawn towards sports. I was on the school football team—and even got chosen for the nationals—the athletics team, the throwball team, etc. Suddenly, I began to view food differently. I became conscious of eating healthier with the objective of growing stronger and training harder. People who follow me on Instagram know that I am a big Stallone fan. One of my first Instagram posts was made to wish him on his birthday. I have his autograph on one of my *Cosmopolitan* cover shoots. I've watched *Rocky*, *II*, *III*, *IV* and *V* a million times. I loved the way he looked, his physique and his no-nonsense attitude. There's a scene in *Rocky 1* where he wakes up in the morning wearing tiny hot-pants and goes to the fridge. He breaks a few raw eggs into a glass and drinks it neat. I was determined to follow in his footsteps. So I began to imitate him. At first, I had to pinch my nose shut because of the foul smell, but gradually, I developed a taste for it. It made me stronger. Even though my sports teacher would encourage us to include more eggs in our diet, I did it mostly for Stallone. I would also eat bananas every morning and go for athletics practice. I was very diligent about this.

And there was my dance. Indian classical dance performances can be very demanding. It was here that

I learnt discipline and to improve my stamina. As I progressed with my dance practice, I learnt to eat right. You cannot eat a heavy meal if you're going to be onstage for two to two and a half hours. If you do, you'll throw up. Being onstage can also make you very thirsty. So I learnt little tricks, like eating a handful of raisins before going onstage. Raisins help to retain moisture in the mouth and keep your mouth hydrated.

Of course, all of this didn't mean that I didn't indulge myself as a child with vada pavs and Frankies and, of course, chocolate. I have a huge sweet tooth and was known to eat an ice cream—chocobars and strawberry-vanilla sticks—a day during lunch break. Even today, every time my husband travels abroad, he's under strict instructions to bring back a small suitcase of chocolates.

Soon, I began to work in films and work played a huge role in shaping me towards being a healthy eater. Suddenly, I became conscious and even extra cautious about what I ate. Before, I didn't care about food, I would eat for the sake of doing so, but things changed once I hit the films. In fact, this was one of the turning points in my life as far as food is concerned. Being in front of the camera demands extra care. Your skin, the way you look, feel, your energy levels, your approach towards your day-to-day life, getting up early . . . everything depends on what you feed into your system. And the roles I took up demanded it. I had a couple of excellent guides to help me navigate my fitness routines and diet.

Even today, through two pregnancies, I still follow these people blindly. My trainer, Satyajeet Chaurasiya, and Shabana Sabherwal, who played a huge role in shaping me into the *Dhoom* girl, getting me the fit washboard abs and toned body. He trained and transformed me in six months into my super-hot avatar. Then, there's Shonali Sabherwal who has been my dietician right from the beginning. She knows exactly what I like eating. And even though she's put me on a complete vegan diet a couple of times for different roles, I was shocked to find that I really enjoyed the food, which consisted of lots of smoothies, berry and fruit bowls to combat the heat so you don't feel lethargic on set. This must be said: I have never permanently been on a diet because I feel starved. I need to eat a proper, solid meal to survive otherwise I get irritated, moody or angry and I can't afford that on set. Besides, both my cook and I have been trained by her. She would also send me dabbas of macrobiotic food—the philosophy of diet as first developed by George Ohsawa in Japan—that she'd made herself. That was when I really started enjoying eating healthy stuff because I had a motive, an incentive, something to look forward to. I, like most people, need a reason for doing something in life because that's when I truly enjoy doing it. Without a reason, I don't really care.

Today, I still eat healthy food, except on Sundays when I let my hair down.

As you can see from my food journey, eating has never been a focal point in my life. Food was something I needed for sustenance, for nourishment, for my sports and for my life in front of the camera. However, now, I'm at another turning point in my life, where food and eating has once again come under the microscope, taking on a bigger, more personal connotation. The perspective has changed. With two toddlers to feed, I've begun to view food in a completely different light. I've looked back at my beginnings to examine all the things I did right and the ones that were wrong. I've begun to question my childhood self: What made me a fussy eater? Why wasn't food interesting or appealing to me? And there have been two major food-related solutions that I've gleaned from my story.

First, food should be fun. All through my childhood, eating came with a barrage of threats, and so, naturally I viewed it as a chore, akin to bathing. Meals were something one *had to do*. Today, most parents have a busy daily schedule and are usually pressed for time. However, one should never resort to threats and blackmail when it comes to feeding a toddler. These are a child's most impressionable years—when life-long habits, likes and dislikes, are programmed into a human being. To raise a healthy and happy child, habits of nutritious and healthy eating must be set right now. Today, if I ever catch anyone trying to threaten or hurry my elder daughter, Radhya, to eat, I immediately correct them. I tell them never to force her; that she'll eat when she wants to; I tell them to ask her a little later if she'd like to try a bite. And, in turn, Radhya is not fussy. She enjoys eating and even during her moody moments, she'll happily eat a whole bowl of curd without any fuss and without needing to be coerced. She never has to fear the hapus-wallah or the bogeyman. And I want her to grow up just like that: completely fearless.

The second point, of course, is variety. Introduce your toddler to the many tastes and textures that food has to offer. And in return, they will thank you for it by enjoying food in its totality. It can be difficult to experiment with a multitude of cuisines and that is why, later in the book, I share with you a host of tried and tested recipes that you can attempt. Remember, at this stage of a child's growth, they are curious about the world and the many experiences it has to offer. They want to experience new sensations, feelings, tastes, sounds and people. Give them the option.

Of course, today I miss the traditional south Indian food that was once made at home, and in retrospect, I've learned that the food I ate as a child couldn't have been healthier. But, at the same time, it took me a long time to come to food with the openness and inquisitiveness that I see in my daughters. Eventually, I did. It took love to get me there . . .

2

What's Love Got to Do with It?

Every year, Jamnabai Narsee would host the most happening event of the school calendar—the Cascade. Students from many different schools would flock to it to participate in various events like art competitions, dance offs, etc. As a twelve-year-old girl, it was the highlight of me and my friends' year. We looked forward to it tremendously. And with good reason. Because it was here that I first met my husband, Bharat. He was tall, good-looking and I immediately had a miserable crush on him.

We ended up sitting beside each other, making awkward conversation; I had butterflies in my stomach and found myself inexplicably drawn to him. Back then, in my braces and high ponytail, I had zero inkling that the universe had a transformative surprise waiting for me. That day, when we exchanged phone numbers on tissue papers, little did we know that in the future we'd be happily married to each other.

But you must be wondering what my love story has to do with feeding one's baby. Will you be surprised if I say *everything*? It is probable that you would not be reading this book had I not met Bharat that fateful day in the 1990s. So lend me your ear, and in no time, all things shall be made clear!

Back in the day, dating was a simple, yet very complicated, affair. Those were the days without smartphones or WhatsApp to connect in an instant or Google and Facebook to look up your crush. We were the generation that had to rely on word of mouth and good old fashioned manual dialling. And dating for me, mostly involved sneaking into my mother's room to use her landline so I could speak to Bharat, while he made it a point to come to all our school events so we could hang out together. We spent a lot of time staring at one another, laughing and giggling. I was just happy that I had this wonderful guy beside me, that we were walking and talking together. We just about held hands, which was a big deal back then!

When I turned eighteen and began working on my first film, things changed. Love and romance took a backseat. Working in the Indian film fraternity is time and energy consuming. There's absolutely no time for a relationship.

In all those years, I'd probably dated only twice, that too very briefly, and they were far from concrete relationships. However, I would often find myself wondering about Bharat and what he was doing. Even though many years had flown by since I'd last seen him, he, strangely, occupied a place in my heart. One day, our paths crossed once again, and after that, there was no looking back.

What was supposed to be casual dinner-and-drinks ended up being a whole night of laughter and conversation. It was the beginning of a completely new chapter in my life. Reconnecting after so many years, we had much to catch up on. After all these years we still connect on many levels and that's what I find beautiful about our relationship. Much later, the next day, as a soft dawn broke over the city sky, we found ourselves still glued to the couch, our conversation far from the finish line. And I realized that I could do this with Bharat every day, again and again, on repeat.

In many ways, this was the turning point in my life. Both my love for Bharat and for food grew together, hand-in-hand. Love can do that to you. Even though we are very similar as people, our histories differ. Bharat is a very sociable Bandra boy who loves life and, especially, food. He introduced me to a whole new world. Being a foodie, he helped me discover a different side of myself, which I never knew existed. He helped me peel back the layers to reveal my hidden talents and passion. However, for this new adventure, my wardrobe—which usually consisted of casual, boring, post pack-up pyjamas or *ganji*s and shorts—needed urgent transformation! I desperately needed date night outfits because there were many dates in the immediate future. Very soon, I realized that colour had started to seep into my usually black wardrobe and it was a refreshing sight.

Food and eating are pivotal during dates, that early period, because it's usually during meals, date lunches and dinners, that a couple really bonds. And Bharat took me to some of the best restaurants and places, opening me up to new cuisines and tastes I'd never tried before. At all these places, he knew exactly what to order. We ate Japanese, Thai, Goan—we went on long drives around the city, stopping for bhutta, eating at the cozy little Chinese joint, Ling's Pavilion, in Colaba. He taught me how to use chopsticks. One day, while I was shooting at Mehboob Studio, Bharat, who was at Yoko—a restaurant in Bandra—with his friends, packed a sizzler and brought it to my vanity van, reviving a taste that I'd forgotten many, many years ago. Even today, it's still our favourite food joint and my mouth waters at the very mention of it. In our relationship there are no flowers and teddy bears. In fact, if I get flowers from Bharat, I'll start to think there's something terribly wrong with him! It's always been through food that we show our love for each other. So the excitement of reconnecting, talking and being in love only grew with good food, and made me look at food with fresh eyes. And suddenly, food was stimulating, exciting, sensual even.

Bharat comes from a big, loving Sindhi family of foodies who enjoy cooking and having meals together. And as you already know, in my family, food was sustenance, not something we fussed over a lot. Bharat lives in a huge joint family in Bandra that is bustling with chachas, *chachi*s and children. It's kind of like a scene from *Hum Saath-Saath Hain*, only that here they all have their separate floors. Visiting his family made me realize what an important role food plays in Bharat's life. On Sundays, you can smell Sindhi kadi and tuk as you enter the building. His mother is a fabulous cook who pampers him with home-made Sindhi delicacies for lunch and dinner, chai and biscuits in the morning and a glass of milk Roo Afza at night—so spoilt, I know! I also realized that good food makes him really happy and when he hasn't eaten well, he's not his usual cheerful self. It made me take notice and think. The many times he'd stayed over at my place—and since I hadn't told anyone that I was dating him, he'd also sneak out first thing in the morning, before my family awoke!—all I could offer him was a cup of instant coffee or whatever fruit was lying around. Bharat is the only guy who has had the good fortune to be invited for a sleepover at my place, and I would soon realize how different our morning routines were.

Bharat enjoys having a leisurely cup of chai at his own pace in the mornings, whereas, back then, I was the kind of person who would get up, shower, pour a cup of coffee, eat an omelette and head to work. Ever so often, I'd eat the omelette in the car itself. In my life, except for when I was in school, there was no sitting down at the table for breakfast. In fact, I rarely even used my kitchen, which looked more like a mock set at a shoot. I mean, I actually used my oven to store things like gifts, cutlery and junk food! That's how pathetic I was. Seeing him at home, his mother fussing over him, I began to feel sorry for the guy. Here I was, offering instant coffee to a guy who wasn't even a coffee drinker. Poor him! So I decided to take matters in my hands.

The first thing I learnt was to make proper Indian chai. My house help, Bharti, who had figured out that something was going on between me and Bharat, told me with a cheeky smirk, '*Mujhe malum hai aapko kyun seekhna hai chai banana. Mai sikhati hun aapko* [I know why you want to learn how to make tea. I'll teach you.]' And one day, to his surprise, Bharat woke up to a cup of chai, just the way he liked it. It's safe to say he was more than impressed because he knew I had done it out of love. He also knew that there was no chance in hell any other guy could have gotten me to learn something I didn't want to do. For me, and perhaps you too, I will break barriers, go that extra mile, for a person I really truly love.

Gradually, with the help of many, many invaluable YouTube videos, I began to try my hand at cooking. The first dish I attempted was Bharat's favourite—Goan prawn curry. I sourced a bottle of authentic Goan masala from my hairstylist, Fatima. If I was going to do something new, I was going to do it properly. Soon, I was working my way through more complex and interesting dishes like crepes, steamed salmon wrapped in banana leaf and Thai curries. Which was amazing for someone who always got confused if she had to fry or boil a potato, right? Needless to say, there were some major flops in the beginning and many instances where I burnt the food to hell and beyond. But one needs to make mistakes to learn, and it takes many to actually cook well.

Time flew by, and I began to enjoy cooking. I noticed that Bharat was now asking me to make things he liked, and soon, we were inviting people over for meals. At times, he too would be next to me in the kitchen, trying his hand at something. Slowly, the kitchen began to look and smell like a real kitchen—*really good*. I enjoyed using all my utensils and began to scour online stores for cooler stuff that would help me be more efficient. To my surprise, I discovered that I was a rather good cook, something

I would've never known if I hadn't fallen in love. Bharat is a humble, hard-working and honest man with simple needs and if I could keep him happy with some good food, I was obviously going to give it my best shot.

They say love is blind but being with Bharat made me open my eyes. There have been so many learning moments during our time together, and I am still learning from and about him. Holidays, in particular, took us out of our comfort zones, where many aspects can remain camouflaged—and made us reveal our inner selves to each other. In Goa, which I'd only visited for film shoots, Bharat introduced me to shacks and authentic Goan food. We went to New York in the winter, and I had never seen the city so white before. In Barcelona, we strolled down quiet alleyways, eating local delicacies like bombas, Spanish cheese and calcots. Our trip to Australia was one giant food fest where we dined at the best Michelin starred restaurants. For our honeymoon to the south of France, we ditched regular restaurants for street food and binged on fried artichokes and ratatouille. And for one of our anniversaries, Bharat took me to Bangkok on a dinner date to a rooftop restaurant on a skyscraper called Vertigo, where the food was beyond divine.

Of course, I also learnt tremendously from his mother and his family. But that being said, I will never attempt cooking Sindhi food because that's his mother's territory and I'm not a fool to go up against a pro!

When we got married in 2012, there were many things that changed. Most of it was for the better. I became more mature, responsible. Of course, once I began living with his family, I couldn't roam around the house in my shorts and ganjis like I used to. But Bharat's family is wonderful and took me into their fold effortlessly. All the women in the Takhtani household are exceptionally good cooks; they are the queens of the kitchen, packing delicious *khane ka dabbas* for their husbands. I, on the other hand, had never cooked a single thing before I'd met Bharat. So I am extremely thankful that I am blessed with a sweetheart of a mother-in-law, who pampered me and never insisted that I enter the kitchen or do any of the orthodox things she had been made to do as a *bahu* (daughter-in-law). In fact, she always tells me that I am like her third son (after Bharat and his brother). And since I was the first bahu in the house, I was pampered rotten. Someone was always sending me chocolate brownies and fruit and cream.

Bharat's family spoilt me so thoroughly that in the first six months of being married, I put on an insane amount of weight! Never before had I seen such a number on the weighing scale. I had gone from omelettes cooked in olive oil to Sunday breakfasts of vada pav and samosas! There were bound to be some consequences. That's when

I decided enough was enough. I had floated on cloud nine for too long. It was time to get back to reality and my old routine—time to call in my trainer and nutritionist. As I switched back to my old eating patterns, I noticed that my habits were beginning to inspire the people around me. Soon, I found my mother-in-law incorporating some of my techniques and ideas, like steamed and grilled food, into their routines and that made me extremely happy.

Don't get me wrong. I love Sindhi cuisine, but it tends to be very rich with lots of fried, oily stuff—papads and chidwas. It wasn't sustainable; after all, I had worked my butt off to get to the figure that you saw onscreen, back during the days of *Dhoom*. I didn't want to flush all that work down the loo! As I resumed eating healthy, Bharat too was encouraged to join in. Even before we'd met, he'd always kept up a healthy fitness and diet routine, but this time around we were doing it together. My biggest achievement of all was to get him to start liking the raw vegetable juice that I drink first thing in the morning. The juice consists of equal parts karela (bitter gourd), doodhi (bottle gourd), beetroot, carrot, tomato and a dash of black salt. It's far from delicious, but it's good for the skin, immunity and digestion. I believe that some parts of life that are good for you, like working out and eating healthy food, are not always easy or pleasant. Life isn't always a bed of roses. But you've got to do what you've got to do!

Pregnancy is altogether different. When I found out that I was pregnant with my first child, it was the most beautiful moment of our lives. Bharat and I were more than ready to welcome a child into this world and take full responsibility for her. I was both excited and nervous, but I knew I wanted to enjoy this phase to the fullest. And being a Scorpio, the zodiac known for its curious and inquisitive nature, I immediately began research and bought a bunch of books to read. In fact, today I have a veritable library of pregnancy books at home! At the same time, I also sought out my guruji's—Amma Bhagvan—advice, and he told me something extremely simple but critical.

His philosophy is: the mother shapes the child. It's as simple as that.

What he means by this is that what you do during your nine months can affect and mould the child you are going to bring into this world. So, as pregnant mothers, we need to stay calm, surround ourselves with happy people and their radiant positivity and keep busy with what brings us contentment and joy. That's exactly what I did, and I urge you to do the same; I've seen the magic behind this philosophy—twice. The first nine months of my pregnancy (and I suspect it is the same for you) were the most important nine months of my whole life. The first pregnancy is always special because everything about it is new and exciting. But the second time I was pregnant, Radhya, my first-born, kept me on my toes.

The first time, I had maintained a pregnancy journal about what I was experiencing, eating and feeling. It came in handy during my second pregnancy. And I strongly suggest you do the same. You don't have to write a book the length of *War and Peace*, just short notes about your observations will suffice. You'll be surprised at how helpful it can be in future.

Really, truly, enjoy your first pregnancy: surround yourself with happy people, make your space clean and comfortable, find the time to pamper yourself (salon visits will be difficult, if not impossible, once your baby arrives). If you have any bad habits, kick them in the butt the day you find out you're pregnant. Instead, focus on making this time exciting for yourself. Do what you love. Even though today there are millions of options to help us unwind on Netflix and Hotstar and whatnot, I went back to my favourite show, *Friends*, and binge-watched it. Listen to music that infuses a sense of lightness into your being. Participate in events you're interested in. Do crafts, cook, write, swim . . . whatever takes your fancy.

My most important piece of advice is: eat well so that you can properly nourish the child in your womb. I didn't restrict myself and didn't care about the weight I was going to pack in. I was confident about my body and in my ability to reboot and get back to the figure I've always had. I had the clarity of thought to understand that if I wanted to have a healthy baby, I needed to eat healthy food—food that is necessary for a pregnant woman. And I pat myself on the back for having done it. Today, I see a lot of mothers who worry about weight gain during their nine months. To them I say: it's normal and inevitable; these changes are bound to happen. Everything is going to expand and grow because there are so many changes that are happening inside your body. Your butt is going to become ten times bigger than Kim Kardashian's or Jennifer Lopez's. Things will change, and you can't look the same. Instead, feel blessed that you have the power to become a mother. You can get back your figure with a little hard work post-delivery; it's all in your hands after all.

And most definitely—banish the word 'diet' during your pregnancy. Eat sensibly and feed your child well. You will find that your child will come into the world with a palate preference. For example, I ate a lot of rasam and curd during my pregnancy, and when Radhya was just a one-year-old, she snatched a bowl of rasam out of my hands and guzzled it. How do you explain that? Rasam has a complicated and spicy taste, not something toddlers normally enjoy. The only reason I can think of why Radhya enjoys the taste so much is that she inherited this love from me. In fact, my mother also ate the same thing when she was carrying me. I like to think that our love for these dishes have been passed down through generations, like stories, from my mother to me and now to my baby girls. In this book, I'm sharing a baby-friendly recipe for rasam. Do give it a try. However, if you're still not convinced about the weight gain, let me tell you about my mother's pregnancy; it will inspire you.

When she was five months pregnant, my mother was shooting for two films—*Satte Pe Satta* and *Razia Sultan*. In the song, 'Dukki Pe Dukki Ho', you can clearly see her bump. That's me in there! And for *Razia Sultan*, she had to ride a horse while pregnant. She tells me that I'm restless and energetic because she was physically active during her nine months. She also danced onstage during her pregnancy. You must remember that she was doing this during the 1980s, when it was radical for a woman to be so active while pregnant. My mother is a superwoman like that, who has always broken the rules and stereotypes of what women should be like. She has always inspired me to push the limits. In fact, I will never forget what she told me when I was pregnant. She said, 'You're not sick that you need to rest all the time. You're simply pregnant. After delivery, your body is at its most elastic and flexible. You can mould it into any shape you want.' And so I followed her advice unconditionally. I performed the dance ballet, *Ramayana*, on stage; I worked on a short film called *Cakewalk*; I wrote this book during my second pregnancy; and I had many other projects in the pipeline. Channelling your inner creativity is a great way to enrich your nine months because the energy and positivity will most certainly be transferred to your child.

That being said, no two pregnancies are alike. If you have complications or have been advised rest by your gynaecologist, do so. Be cautious. Don't be silly or impulsive. From the day you know you're pregnant, you must be careful. There will be many people with all sorts of advice during this time but pay heed to only one person: your gynaecologist. If you ever find yourself confused about any aspect of your pregnancy, go to your gynaecologist. Kiran S. Coelho was my gynaecologist and best friend during both my pregnancies. She understood me, made me feel comfortable, listened to my innumerable questions and also told me to stop stressing. In fact, she once very sweetly told me: 'Stop reading so much and just relax!' Find a gynaecologist who will not only give you the confidence to go through this period but will also be your pillar of support.

Finally, I went to Greece on a babymoon with my husband. We spent time on the magical islands of Santorini, Mykonos and Athens. Having worked in so many films where I had to romance heroes—or be romanced—at beautiful locales, I too wanted my dream photoshoot to capture my pregnancy with my very own, real life hero, Bharat. I wanted to capture and preserve the moment forever. I wanted those precious photos to adorn the walls of my home.

My manager, Pamela, researched many photographers in Santorini and finally put us in touch with the brilliant Dimitris Psillakis, who scheduled our shoot in time for the sunrise. This time around, Bharat and I were our own stylists, make-up men, spot-boys—we even ironed each other's clothes. After the shoot, Dimitris was shocked to learn that I'm an actress back home and asked me why I hadn't told him before. I told him that I was there as a mother, not an actress. I wanted to remember the moment as a personal one, completely cut off from the usual professional moorings. Our boutique hotel was located in a sleepy little village that went to bed rather early. So of course, there was nothing to eat . . . for miles. Another night in Santorini and I woke up starving, irritated and in a bad mood. Bharat and I sleepily trudged through country roads in search of food. And to make matters worse, it began to pour cats and dogs! Finally, after what seemed like a lifetime, we found a taverna that still had its lights on. We asked if they were still serving. Noticing me, the chef, an Italian gentleman, readily agreed and asked us what we'd like to eat. It turned out that he, too, had a pregnant wife and could surmise what I was going through, shooting

Bharat a quick knowing look. That night, under the glassy, star-speckled Grecian sky, drenched to the bone, I had the best spaghetti bolognaise of my life.

My babymoon had a domino effect; the pictures were a big hit on social media. And soon, fathers-to-be were reprimanding Bharat for starting this trend. 'What have you done!' they admonished him. 'Now my wife wants the same. You've just increased our expenses!'

I won't swap my experiences of being pregnant for anything in the world. And neither should you because this is your special time. Make it perfectly, personally yours by doing what you find exciting, yet comfortable. Cherish it. In any case, it will be the only 'me-time' you'll have before your baby arrives . . .

3

Bringing Baby Home

In my entire life, *the* most magical and wondrous moment I've ever experienced was when I became a mother, first with Radhya and then with Miraya.

Bharat was there beside me, misty-eyed, when the doctor placed Radhya in my arms. She put her mouth on mine, and as I drank in her sweet baby breath, feeling her tender skin against mine, I felt—for the very first time—pure 100 per cent, unadulterated, unalloyed love and my heart exploded with joy. In a heartbeat, she had transformed me from a daughter into a mother. Now, I was the lioness and she, my little cub. I was going to protect and love this baby for the rest of my life.

The only other time I feel this sense of closeness is when I am with my mother, lying on her lap or hugging her. Yet, this feeling of oneness was at a different, inexplicable level. It was both intense and primal, tender and spiritual.

And those first few moments changed me forever. I was now a mother, and it was an amazing feeling. How blessed and lucky women are to experience this almost divine, yet natural and powerful feeling! When I had my second baby, Miraya, I once again felt this powerful wave of emotions. It's still special, even though the first time has a novelty factor. Having had my baby girls, I realized that I love how they make me feel, that I adore being a mother, that I can do it over and over again just to re-live those first few precious moments. Really, hold your newborn and cherish every second because it's the most blessed feeling in the world.

When I stepped out of Hinduja Hospital after both my deliveries, I was greeted by a host of media and well-wishers who were patiently waiting for a glimpse of the baby. I extend all my gratitude to them for always showing me so much love as an artist. Back home, both my baby girls have always been welcomed with a beautifully decorated house—pink balloons, bouquets of flowers and gifts from my friends and family. I still remember those days as if they happened just yesterday. The first few weeks of bringing baby home are simply beautiful. My first baby, Radhya, came home in October, just as Diwali was starting. The streets and buildings were magically lit and there were sounds of crackers going off everywhere. It seemed like the whole world had conspired to throw her a big welcome party! My second baby, Miraya, came home in the monsoon in June to the sound of gentle soothing rain. Both times, our parents greeted them with a little ritual—an *aarti* and a tika—and then they were taken to the nursery, which had been spruced, cleaned and tidied with new bedding and clothes waiting for them.

The atmosphere during the first few weeks of bringing the baby home is always very peaceful, loving and pleasant, like a fairy tale. There's the soft gurgling of the baby in the nursery, one of my favourite songs, 'Sweet Lullaby', playing gently in the background, everyone speaks softly and is extra cautious around the newborns. In the evenings, I would set aside time for well-wishers, friends and family who would drop by to see the baby, bringing gifts and warmth. Then there are messages from friends and people I work with, wishing us the best. Visitors are awed by this atmosphere of calm and peace as they coo over the newborn, and yet . . .

Little do they know that this peace is all on the surface.

If you get a glimpse into my head (or any new mothers') at this precise moment, you will find that it's a completely different story. There's only one word for it: chaos! Of course, it has nothing to do with the baby; she is the most precious. The madness that ensues in a woman's mind during this time is affected by many external factors and one of the biggest culprits (besides the raging hormones) is usually *other people*. Let me explain.

If I told you the number of times a person (strangers even!) have come up to me and ladled me with some advice, you'd be exhausted counting. From the time my babies have come into this world (and sometimes even *before* my delivery) all I've heard is advice, advice and more advice. And all of it is unwarranted. Long-lost relatives who've not spoken to me in ages suddenly resurface, like meerkats armed with questions. Their attack usually follows a few distinctive weapons, such as:

How are you sitting like this?

Tumhara normal tha ki C-sec? (Did you have a normal delivery or a C-section?)

Are you getting enough milk? (This was asked after an intense session of my breasts being stared at!)

Why don't you feed your baby *this*?

Why don't you give her *that*?

Why don't you cut her hair now?

Why did you cut her hair so short?

You must *not* feed her this!

You *must* feed her that!

—and on and on and on, till I was ready to explode.

Their nosy and insensitive behaviour is one of the main reasons I was on the edge during those early months. Pregnancy and delivery are extremely personal. Remember, all decisions regarding your child should only be taken by you, in consultation with your partner, and for medical and technical queries, your doctor. *No one else.*

Then there's the advice from random people on social media. I would not call them my fans or well-wishers. I'm talking about the trolls on the Internet who always have something nasty to say, no matter what you do. There was, for example, '*How do you actresses lose weight so quickly after childbirth??!!*' Or '*Concentrate on your kids and not the parlour!*' They forget that I've invested years of time and hard work into sculpting my body, that I'm fit, that I can get back on a training schedule much more quickly than others who haven't been as physically active. But there's no winning with these guys! As a mother who is also a public persona, it can sometimes be hard to listen to or read about judgemental and nasty comments online. However, luckily for me, I've been in the film industry from a very young age and so, I've developed a thick skin and don't get affected by what is said on the Internet. But I can see how questions and unsolicited advice and the lack of privacy can affect a new mother's mental health, cause depression and anxiety and even lead to self-doubt.

On top of this, a new mother is almost always a mad multi-tasker. She must not only care for and feed her child, but also manage and look after her house, her husband, the help *and* her work. Even though the month before a woman's delivery involves a lot of planning, prepping and shopping for the baby who is going to arrive, once you do bring the baby home you realize there are millions of little things that you missed out. Also, as a new mother, there are many necessities you would've never thought of, which only experience will teach you—buckets, bottles, jugs, diapers, clothes stands . . . the list is always seemingly endless. And soon you find yourself perpetually calling your local store because something is always, and always urgently, required.

And if you already have a baby in the house, you also have to ensure that your first child is being well looked after. When I had my second baby, I had to be doubly careful about balancing the scales and giving both the attention they deserve. I had to make sure that my eldest was equally happy and that she was comfortable about having a sister. I needed to be certain that my first child accepted the new baby in the house and did not feel jealous in any way. Thankfully, Radhya is an ideal elder sister. She loves Miraya. She is always kissing her baby sister and talking to her. Considering all of this, a new mother definitely has a lot on her hands.

Yet these are all superficial. The real problems run deeper. Most women who've just had a baby go through a terrifying emotional roller-coaster, which varies in intensity from one individual to another. Post-partum depression is not a myth. After my first delivery, I sailed through my recovery, and it made me wonder why some of the women I knew often found themselves feeling low after their deliveries. But after my second delivery, there were times when I too felt like shutting myself in an empty room or bursting into tears without any reason. Luckily, my mother noticed my short period of post-partum depression. She saw how, in a room filled with people, I would be lost in my own world, totally removed from the conversations around me. I was feeling very hollow, empty. And suddenly I'd feel like crying when I had absolutely no reason to do so. It annoyed me that I couldn't pinpoint the reason behind this emotional upheaval. My mother advised me to consult my doctor immediately and nip the problem in the bud. Blood tests revealed the answers. My hormone levels were completely out of whack and my doctor immediately put me on certain vitamins and medicines. It took me a couple of weeks to get back to my usual self. Once the hormone levels had evened out, I automatically started to feel better and more like my usual self. Women who feel depressed after their delivery should know that it isn't their fault or the fault of the people around them. The reason is fluctuating hormones. Urban mothers are fortunate that they have a wealth of knowledge at their disposal. But this awareness must be taken to rural areas to guide women who may not be privy to this information to help them through this complicated time.

'In fact, it is quite common,' says Dr Suneeta Banerjee, MBBS, GGO, functional medical doctor at Health Aesthetics. 'In America, one in seven patients suffer and in India it's on the rise. About 22 per cent of all Indian women suffer from it.'

That's a surprising statistic, right? So what exactly is postnatal depression?

'Immediately after giving birth to a baby, a mother can go into a state of happiness or she can also suffer from post-partum depression,' says Dr Suneeta. 'She may have feelings of sadness, fearfulness, anxiety. She may feel hopeless, worthless and very lonely. It can happen immediately after delivery or take a few weeks to develop and it usually lasts between six to eight weeks, after which it settles down. But in some cases post-partum depression can continue. When these symptoms continue or get worse, then it is time she seeks a doctor's help so as to be treated correctly. If not treated, she can suffer from post-partum depression for three years after childbirth and even later on in life.

'After childbirth, a woman's hormones suddenly change. Women have two main hormones—oestrogen and progesterone, and both these levels become high during pregnancy to support the foetus. Immediately after childbirth, progesterone levels drop drastically to the pre-pregnancy state, while oestrogen levels remain the same. So there is a difference between the levels between these two hormones and we call this "oestrogen dominance (ED)". And this difference in the levels is what causes post-partum depression. ED can also affect the thyroid and adrenalin glands and can cause one to feel low. Also, there are other hormones like prolactin, which is secreted after childbirth so that the woman can feed her baby, and this also causes emotional disturbances in women. So because of all these factors and fluctuations, a woman can suffer post-partum depression.'

So what should a woman do to combat post-partum depression?

'First and foremost, she should eat a rich, nutritious diet,' says Dr Banerjee. 'She should have plenty of fruits, nuts, and meats if she is a non-vegetarian. She must have iron and calcium tablets. And it's very important to take Omega 3. If she is a vegetarian, flax seed oil is a great option. Secondly, exercise is very important because it has been proven that it has an anti-depressant effect because physical activity releases happy endorphins that reduce the stress hormone—cortisol. Daily walks are a good way to include light exercise into one's routine. Thirdly, sleep is crucial because it gives the body an opportunity to rest and recover. Research has shown that those women who get the least amount of sleep (less than four hours, between midnight to 6 a.m. and even less than an hour during the day) suffer the maximum symptoms of depression. So that's why they say—*sleep when the baby sleeps*. Fourthly, breastfeeding can also reduce the effects of post-partum depression. A new mother needs all the help she can get from her family so she can recover both emotionally and physically.'

Women are definitely the braver of the two sexes. Childbirth is exceptionally natural and complicated all the same. Plus, there's the physical exhaustion. New mothers never get any sleep because they need to look after their child's needs and, most importantly, feed them. It's as if we are perpetually jet-lagged. And because I am extra cautious, and slightly OCD about everything, after my first delivery, I took it upon myself to do everything myself, even though I had an excellent nurse. In fact, I spent a lot of time keeping an eye on the nurse to see if she was doing everything correctly! However, the second time around I was more confident. I hired the same nurse who had taken care of Radhya, and since I knew her, I trusted her enough to keep my nerves calm. Round two is always a bit more relaxing because you are not charting unexplored waters. You've done it before. The only challenge is that now you have two babies to look after instead of one. But there's nothing we women cannot do.

That is why I feel it is critical for new mothers, after a few weeks have passed, to find a way to leave the house, even if it's for an hour or two, to start reconnecting with the normal course of her life. Of course, it goes without saying that the child should be left with a responsible person in-charge while you are away. But getting out is good for your mental health. After both my deliveries, I made it a point to make time for a dinner date with my husband and it felt like a breath of fresh air because otherwise, all through my waking hours as a new mother, I'd be wrapped up in baby world, with no thought to what I ate, wore or did. Most times, I roamed around the house without even running a brush through my hair! So a few weeks after I had had my second baby, I went to the salon to get my hair coloured. It was my way of unwinding and reconnecting with myself. But guess what happened? I posted a picture of me in the salon and I got trolled for not being a responsible mother!

Self-care is super important after childbirth. It can be difficult and challenging in the first few weeks, when you feel like you have the weight of the whole world on your shoulders, to make time for yourself. But you need to try and find a way to carve out some space for yourself by doing whatever it is that you like to do. When I finally went out with my husband for dinner, it felt wonderful to touch base with him and even better to get into something that wasn't maternity wear (which I'd packed and kept ready for my sister or sister-in-law's round two)! These moments made me feel like myself again.

But this doesn't mean that I wasn't tired or zoned out most of the time when I was at home. Since I breastfed both my daughters, I inevitably felt exhausted and hungry all the time. As a mother, feeding your baby is an intimate and warm experience, a moment of bonding between you and your child. I learnt a lot about both my daughters during these moments together. I ensured that I was eating nutritious food during this phase. In fact, I put on more weight while I was feeding my babies than when I had been pregnant. But I wasn't worried about it. My diet consisted of nutrient-rich pulses and lentils like nachni, dalia, dry fruits, fruits and tons of methi ladoos, which are fantastic for a feeding mother. My mother-in-law also gave me a wonderful and natural supplement, rich in fat and protein, that had also worked tremendously well for her. The supplement consisted of ground badam (almond), mishri (sugar) and elaichi (cardamom), which was powdered into a fine texture in the blender. I would have a spoonful of it whenever I was hungry or sprinkle it over my porridge for breakfast. I also had some wonderful and nourishing pomegranate juice that my nurse would give me, which is great for breastfeeding mothers.

There are many benefits of breastfeeding your child, however, I see many women who have trouble doing it or are pressurized into it by family members. Women can go through hell trying to get the process right because it can be painful for them. This can lead to depression and self-doubt. If you're having trouble breastfeeding, see your doctor or lactation specialist—they are the only two people who you should consult and get advice from. If it doesn't work out for you, don't beat yourself up about it. It's not the end of the world. Tell your partner about it and discuss it among yourselves. No one else needs to know because it is a personal choice. In fact, I rarely discuss these issues with my mother, whom I love to bits.

In a blink of an eye, the weeks flew by and soon it dawned on me that I needed to get back to my old routine. Slowly, but steadily, I began to include some light exercises and yoga into my routine. Yoga really helped calm my mind. In fact, immediately after my first pregnancy, I received a very special offer—the chance to perform a solo Odissi show at Siri Fort in New Delhi. The event was only five months after my first delivery, but I couldn't let it slip by. So I grabbed the opportunity and confirmed my participation. *'Can I do it?'* I had asked myself, but I'm a tough nut. I just answered with, *'Bring it on!'*

I began to train hard and in no time, the extra weight began to melt away. Within a couple of months, I began to see changes. I went from a US size 12 to 10 to 8 and finally to a size 2. My transformation was amazing. I thank my dance teacher and trainer for it. And, truth be told, I don't think I've looked better than I ever did till I had my first baby. Today, I can proudly say that I look my best after having become a mother. But I worked hard for it.

Having a goal or an incentive (like I did) helps because it keeps you focused and gives you a something to work towards and a purpose. It is harder to work when you don't have a concrete goal. This is true for most things in life. Try to include some mild exercise into your routine as soon as you're able to. Full body massages, yoga and breathing exercises are a great way to begin. Don't sit for too long and complain that you are putting on weight. Being sedentary after pregnancy will only lead to piling up more weight. Usually, it's best to start slowly and steadily two months after delivery. If you had earlier been working out or going to the gym or had an active physical life before you got pregnant, getting back into shape will be much easier because you already have an in-built framework and muscle in your system. Do inform your trainer about what you went through during your pregnancy and if there were any complications.

All this is possible only after you take some time out from your schedule. It doesn't have to be a whole day. Try to set aside even fifteen minutes a day just for yourself.

Four months after my first delivery, during a workout session where I had also taken Radhya along so I could keep an eye on her, I had an epiphany. I was on the treadmill and a few feet ahead of me was my daughter and her nanny. She was following my baby girl around with a bowl in her hand—coaxing, forcing her to eat. But Radhya wasn't interested; she was more keen to play and just be a toddler. This went on for some time. Then, at one point, I saw her transform from a happy, cheerful baby into a stressed and angry child, lines furrowing her little forehead as she burst out crying. She seemed to not like what was being offered to her. My heart ached with guilt and worry. I stopped my session and rushed to my baby. It was when I was soothing her that I realized that this had to stop. I could not offload the care of my baby onto someone else. I had to be involved, a 100 per cent, actively and responsibly. Yet, I am a working mother who has many professional commitments. For the first time, I felt the tugging conflict spring up between my personal and professional life. It was then that I realized that the only way I would be happy and able to work with freedom is if my baby was happy and content. A happy baby meant a calm and worry-free mother. And to achieve this, I had to take matters into my own hands. I decided that everything—her health, clothes, food, education—would be my sole responsibility. I am glad this awakening happened when it did because Radhya was just starting to develop a taste for and an understanding of food. It meant that I could shape my babies' taste palate and encourage them towards good eating habits.

And the first and most important step towards achieving this was ensuring that she had proper nutritious food that she enjoyed. No more coaxing, cajoling and forcing. That is why I set on a journey to try out, experiment and create the best recipes that would make food fun for children.

As I delved deeper into this mission, I began to revamp my entire kitchen into one more baby-friendly space. This was the second time my kitchen was undergoing a transformation. My favourite coffee maker, which earlier had pride of place, was relegated to the back and my baby's milk bottles, steamers, mixers, sterilizers and cutlery took precedence. Soon, my black-and-white, serious and adult kitchen was transformed into a more baby-proofed, colourful and cheerful space.

During the search for fun and healthy recipes for children, I also ended up speaking to many mothers, nannies, nurses, doctors, paediatricians, friends and house help, who have all found their way into this story. In the process, I was also inspired to improvise and add a modern twist to many age-old recipes. Trepidation and anxiety went hand-in-hand along with the excitement to experiment with baby-friendly recipes, which were safe and also easy to make. I soon realized that I had collected and recorded hundreds of recipes. Today, I am sharing those recipes with you so that you too can benefit from my experience and raise a happy and healthy child. I have consciously made sure to keep things simple with easy prep processes and commonly found ingredients, making sure it is of use to *all* mothers.

One day, as I was whipping up a meal for my babies in the kitchen—lullabies playing in the background, toys scattered everywhere, screams and baby giggles filling the air—I had a fleeting vision, remembering all the times when Bharat and I had begun dating: when we ordered in from restaurants, when I was learning how to cook and sometimes when I'd make a mess of it, when there were friends always pouring in, reheating food in the microwave while entertaining, Bob Marley's reggae and Morrison's rock playing into the wee hours of the morning. How young and restless we were then! I couldn't help but smile.

Today, Bharat's and my life has changed drastically, but only for the better. Our baby girls have brought in colour, cheer and wonder into our lives and I wouldn't trade it for anything in the world.

4

The AHA Moment

Newborn babies are angels when it comes to food.

They lap up pretty much anything they're given, unless they have a bad tummy. Feeding my first born was like being in a dream.

And so, at three months, I, with the help of the nurse, gave her the first taste of food—bottle gourd soup, which had been boiled and strained. The first time we ever attempted making it is a story in itself. I had bought an easy mixer for the purpose of making these soups. The nurse, Sister Jayalakshmi and I were unsure about how to close the lid. The nurse is very independent and likes to do everything on her own, while I, on the other hand, want to help *her* all the time. It's a constant tug of war between us. And more because of it, rather than despite it, we share a lovely relationship and I love her to bits. We thought we had figured out how the mixer worked and gave it a start.

Little did we know that the lid wasn't shut properly and in seconds—there was mashed green doodhi all over the room and on her pristine white uniform that she's very particular about and takes a lot of pride in. After the fiasco, it was aprons for everyone.

Sister Jayalakshmi and I then fed Radhya the doodhi stock with a tiny squeezy spoon, just as her paediatrician, Dr Chittal, had advised. When I saw that she lapped it up so easily, we began to introduce other vegetables (stock only) like beetroot and carrot into her diet. Of course, when to feed your baby their first taste of food varies because every baby is different. Some parents wait till their baby is six months before they introduce them to something other than milk. But I had a hunch that my baby girl was going to be a foodie and I wasn't disappointed.

Gradually, after a couple of months, I moved from liquid to mashed food (in between milk sessions on Dr Chittal's advice). He says, 'It is recommended that the transition from liquid to semi-solid to solid form of food is gradual and continuous. The baby is initially on what is essentially a liquid diet of milk. At around four months of age, semi-liquid and pasty food, such as purees, are started. By the time the child is five months old, you graduate to more grainy textured and solid food.' Do read his advice at the end of the chapter.

At home, mashed peanuts, stewed apple with a dash of cinnamon, stewed pear, avocado with curd, mashed curd rice and mashed pulao were her staples. Once the paediatrician gave me the green light, a little salt was introduced into her diet. I would wait for her to get very hungry and then feed her the mashed food, maintaining a gap of a couple of hours between her milk and the food so that she wasn't overfed, but not too long a gap, that she was agitated or acidic. This was when I also learned that it's good to try and start a routine for the baby as well, and to stick to it as much as possible. Newborns can't tell between day and night. They mark time between hunger and satiation and are dependent on you. So it is up to the parent to introduce them to the safety of a fixed routine. And trust me, your life will be much simpler once you have a routine in place because it will give you your much-needed 'me time'.

Then, finally, one year later there came teeth, the gradual transition to solid food and with that the new food troubles began. This is when most babies begin teething. They are often in pain and feel uncomfortable. This is also the time when a baby begins to develop a hint of individuality, which grows stronger every day. Babies at this age begin to discern between their likes and dislikes, and start to throw tantrums because they instinctively sense that they can get away with it. I was at a loss when one day, my sweet gurgling baby who would guzzle all sorts of vegetable soups and swallow all her mashed foods, dug her heels in. She began to say no to food.

On that fateful day when Radhya threw a tantrum, I had an awakening about both my baby's future and my own. I had earlier decided to take matters into my hands and had taken over full control of my daughter's life. Of course, it was easier said than done. Because how do you take control of the well-being of a bawling, screaming toddler—to boot, one that refuses to eat?

I first realized that Radhya was hard to feed when she did exactly what I had when I had been a child. By the grace of God, Radhya has cute, chubby cheeks. At the same time, it's very hard to tell whether kids with chubby cheeks have swallowed their food or have merely chewed and stored it all in their mouth. One day, we were all sitting together, Radhya was on her feeding table, and the nanny and I were feeding her. I was standing next to the nanny, applauding how swiftly Radhya was eating and enjoying her meal. Little did I know what lay behind those cheeks—a lot of food tucked away, only to be sprayed on the poor nanny! After that day, everyone had aprons on while feeding Radhya.

During my nine months of pregnancy, I had voraciously read every book I could get my hands on—about motherhood and the first year after delivery. I thought I'd have a good handle on the process when my baby arrived. But once she came into this world, it seemed like everything I'd read and learnt had drained out of my brain—like water through a sieve. Certain things I'd read worked for me, but others did not. Troubleshooting baby issues is a lot like a rom-com. Great on film and nice to watch, but completely rubbish in real life. I mean, how many times has a handsome hunk run through the airport to find you just as you're boarding your flight, down on his knees and begging you to marry him? Right? There are some things in life that just don't translate into the real experience of blood, sweat and tears—into real life. And having a baby is on the top of that list. No amount of theory will prepare you for the real event. The only useful tips that worked for me were the ones I ran through with a trial-and-error method. You have to fashion your own ways of doing things and solving problems. You have to be ingenious, creative and intuitive. It's your journey, your battle and your book. So create your own dos and don'ts because each child is different. This is the one job that does not come with a manual. When it comes to a baby, you've got to learn on the job.

And that's exactly what I did. I got to work.

I desperately wanted to understand why my baby was throwing tantrums. So I began with something very simple.

I began to observe her carefully.

For six months I put my life on hold and was present by my daughter's side, asking myself these questions: Why is she crying? What makes her happy about this particular dish that I'm feeding her? Why does the other one agitate her? What makes her smile?

The days passed by. Soon, my daughter was painting me a picture of her likes, dislikes, moods and tantrums. That picture was right in front of me. All I had to do was stop, listen and watch. She was communicating with me in her own little, wordless way and I began to learn her language in a way I'd never learnt anything about her before. I learnt that Radhya was a clever little baby. That she had a varied taste palate. That she didn't like monotony. Or being forced at mealtimes. As the months slid by, she told me other things: she loves milk and that she still is a complete milk baby, she loves cheese and lime, rasam (like me), chiwda and fried food (like her dad). For a moment, I remember thinking how I would've never noticed all these small signs and signals, her own way of reaching out to me, if I hadn't stopped and paid attention.

If you have a toddler who is fussy or hates eating, I would suggest you begin there, by paying attention. Deeply observing your child to hear what she's telling you. They do not have the gift of your language yet, but it's not that they are not communicating with you.

There is no one else who can do this for you. This is your homework; these are the pieces of the puzzle that you will lay out to put together a picture of your child's wonderful and magical personality—a personality that is just beginning to bloom.

And at the same time, you are not the only observer. Your child is doing the very same thing.

With every passing day, your child will observe, absorb, develop, grow, acquire new skills and learn desperately about her/his environment. Most of the time, the reason behind a child's tantrum is boredom. Boredom, teething, lack of sleep or knowledge about the situation they are in or the food they are being given—That's where the problems usually begin when it comes to food. Think about this: babies with bad tummies are usually given khichdi as it is light yet nutritious. But imagine being fed khichdi day after day till your stomach settled down? Boring, right? That's one reason why babies tend to throw major tantrums. During times like these, you can also experiment with a dish like khichdi by adding different ingredients to it. In this book, there are many different types of vegetable khichdi that you can try. Keep boredom at bay and half your job is done. Toddlers will pick up new likes and discard old favourites faster than you can wrap your head around it. My baby girl is too quick for me, too. She's a child who loves variety when it comes to food, and I always have to be on my toes. But to be able to keep up with my child's vibrant taste preferences, I needed to have a plan—a plan that would have my back, keep me sane and two steps ahead of her.

That was the first time I sat down and drew up a monthly meal plan, broken down into weeks. Initially, it took a lot of time and I had to majorly wrack my brains for ideas. I planned it down to the T. No repetitions, no monotony. Every day I put down something new for her to eat. Tweaked old recipes, which I (and my mother, her mother and my mother-in-law) was given as a toddler. When I put the plan into action, I was nervous. What if it backfired? What if I failed? I was already wearily thinking of Plan B. But Radhya took to it like a fish to water. She loved that she had something new to look forward to each day—a new flavour, texture, taste. Mealtimes became exciting, a time of discovery and adventure.

It was while planning her meals that I was struck by the thought—how many million mothers are going through exactly what I am at the moment? How many women are struggling to find ways to feed their babies? If what I was doing for my child could benefit them, wouldn't it be wonderful? And it occurred to me that I *could* reach out to them and help them lay a bit of their burden down since I was already compiling, tweaking, inventing and reinventing recipes for my daughter.

And there's no better medium to reach to people than by writing a book, which would last forever. Mothers from different generations can turn to this book for help and ideas. I started developing these recipes purely because of Radhya. Being with her, spending time with her, seeing her face and her tantrums when she wouldn't eat helped me hone my intuition and craft. My daughter helped me create these simple, fuss-free, down-to-earth recipes; she made me get my brain going, and she definitely made me write this book. And I really thank my beautiful baby for coming into this world and inspiring me to become a writer. She's helped me take charge of her by showing me her beautiful personality. With the help of my brilliant cook, the nanny, the nurse—the power of women—I created this collection of recipes, which has both saved me and satiated my babies. This book doesn't have too many demands, expectations or ingredients. This book is for every mother who wants to get her child to eat and begin to love food.

Okay, back to business.

So I had battled through level one—getting a toddler to eat. But soon I began asking myself yet another question—how was I going to keep her engaged? I wanted her to love food, to come to it of her own volition. I considered what would get a toddler's attention when it involved food? And no, I don't mean the iPad or the TV.

I see many parents resorting to them when it comes to mealtimes or even when they want to keep them quiet for a while. I understand why they do it. It's convenient and easy and after a long day at work, it's a relief to have your child quieten down, even if it's in front of a YouTube video. It's not easy being a parent and smart phones and iPads can be breathers during moments of desperation. That being said, I do believe they are a shortcut, and something I'd like to avoid for as long as it's possible. Too many children today are lonely and insecure because they are intensely connected to the world in a superficial way. And that sad journey usually begins with a phone. Radhya still thinks that my phone can only be used for talking and that there's no other use for it. Of course, my babies have TV time for a short period. It's not like I want them to think the TV is an alien object or grow up technologically challenged, but I don't ever want them to be heavily dependent on technology either. So how was I going to keep my babies engaged without resorting to the easy way?

I found the answers in creativity. Upping the fun quotient is a ridiculously simple task when it comes to toddlers. Especially when they are learning shapes and colours. I bought bird-shaped dosa makers, Mickey Mouse-shaped omelette makers, little flower-shaped pancake pans. Her crockery, too, was brightly coloured. Suddenly, food isn't just about eating because there's play and curiosity involved. During mealtimes, I also bring her a bowl of vegetables to touch, hold, feel, and sometimes nibble at. It gives her something tactile and food-related.

Keeping a child engaged is a mammoth task, but sometimes, the trick of distraction can also help them eat. In my home, it's through the age-old trick of the in-house entertainment team, which comprises me, the nanny and the grandmothers. When my babies are having a bad meal day, we put up a big show for them—dancing, singing, performing, storytelling. It keeps them amused, absorbed and perfectly distracted while we feed them. So include your own trusted family members and people into entertaining your child.

Storytelling is a big part of our entertainment programme. Radhya, Miraya and all babies in general, love to be told stories because it boosts their imagination and takes them on an imaginary adventure. Radhya is hungry for stories. I tell her stories at night, before sleeping, and especially, while eating. The stories are simple and involve her favourite characters. Her favourite tales are always about Darian, my younger sister's son, her cousin. Any story that involves him makes her eyes go big and she readily eats up all her food. So I make up stories about her and Darian going off on an adventure to the jungles where they encounter wild animals. With five Shih Tzus at home—Simba, Betty Boo, Babushka, Cordita and Butterkiss—it's safe to say she loves animals too, and our stories always feature them and her going off on marvellous adventures. Her other favourite character is a kid from her playschool, whom she adores because he's a little smaller than her, and she thinks of him as her little brother. She also loves this girl called Ritik, a couple of years older than her, who comes to play with her during the weekends. One way I can surely get Radhya to eat is if I tell her that Ritik is coming to visit. In a jiffy, the food will all be gone. She also loves stories about her baby sister whom she calls Mia. Storytelling is a creative and simple process that can work wonders when it comes to feeding children. And it's so much better than the TV because it's organic and engaging.

Another thing that seems to work with a fussy eater is giving them a sense of control. Now that Radhya is bigger, she gets her own tiffin and child-friendly cutlery to bring to playschool. I've noticed that she likes to use the fork and spoon to feed herself. She's trying to be independent and take charge of her eating habits. In fact, she also likes to feed me. 'Amma eat, Amma eat,' she'll say while spooning the food into my mouth. I let her do it because the process works through the good old trick of imitation. When your child sees how you are eating, without throwing a fuss, they will internalize the process and reinvent the same motions.

When your toddler is big enough to hold things, try giving them a small bowl filled with what they are eating, and allow them to eat on their own, even while simultaneously feeding them. This will give them freedom and a sense of play and examination. After all, some babies are bosses!

Today there are many schools of parenting and one of them says that you should only feed your child when they are truly, very hungry. However, I think that with babies the early bird truly catches the worm. I believe that a child should have a routine, especially when it comes to mealtimes. And a routine makes life simpler for mothers.

In fact, here's a doctor's perspective:

'Children cannot be relied on to demand food as needed, reliably, in infancy and need to be fed diligently to sustain proper growth, as well as to prevent deficiencies of vitamins and minerals,' says Dr Chittal. 'After two years, they may be fed on demand, making sure the essential nutrients are given adequately and not indulging in junk food if the child so demands.'

I make sure that my babies have four proper meals a day. Breakfast, lunch, a light late afternoon snack and an early dinner, plus a glass of milk before they fall asleep. Babies need the energy and nutrition. If you leave your child alone for an entire day without food, they will suffer from acidity, become cranky and weak. Of course, their intake of food is only outside of their consumption of milk, the ratio of which will change as they grow, the latter increasing. Radhya loves milk; she's a complete milk baby. Sometimes to avoid eating food, she'll try to trick us. '*Mujhe doo doo,*' she'll cry. She does this to avoid eating food. So I, too, am smart about servicing her demands. I give her half a glass, at least an hour before lunch, so that she isn't absolutely full and gives lunch a toss. Now that she's older it's much easy to keep her to a routine, but it's been a slow, long and learning curve. But trust me, you'll get there if you start these habits early.

Another thing to establish is the place the baby will eat. Set up their feeding chair in a single, specific spot to reinforce the idea of routine and place. If you keep shifting places for meals, the child will get distracted with the newness of the space or room and then food will take a backseat.

But sometimes, vary the place by taking your child to a restaurant. It helps them see food in a different light. All around them, they can see people eating and socializing and that can leave a positive impression in their minds about eating. Once, in LA, my husband, the nanny, Radhya and I were at a beautiful restaurant called the Ivy. Radhya was just eight months old and this was the first time I noticed her *noticing* the restaurant. Settled into her feeding chair, she merrily pointed to the breadbasket. When we gave it to her, she took it, broke it into pieces and ate some of the bread. When our dishes arrived, she wanted a taste of everything. It was a pleasure to see her joyous experience of the restaurant. Today, we take our babies out for afternoon lunches to different restaurants because it's a refreshing change. Although we pre-feed them before they head out, they never hesitate to nibble and take a bite of everything at these restaurants!

Finally, and this I've mentioned right at the start of the book, you should never force a fussy eater because it will only drive them away from food. No horror stories or threats either. Don't make eating a scary prospect for them. In fact, you need to do just the opposite.

So there you have it; getting a child or a fussy eater to eat involves work. But it isn't something complicated. Step one: observe your child, their likes and dislikes. Some children like variety, others find comfort in repetition. Try to find out what your child's preferences are. Keeping these in mind, draw up a meal plan. Find ways to entertain your child while feeding them and include the family, prioritize imagination and not the TV. Give your child their sense of control. Engage them with innovative and interesting food or cutlery. And try and stick to a routine that works for you; it will lead to habit formation.

As a first-time mother, there will be challenges, trials and times when you just want to give up. But no journey that's worth its salt is without these ups and downs. Take a deep breath and take comfort in the fact that there are millions of women like you, at this very same moment, trying to work it out too. It's why I wrote this book. This book is my journey as a woman and a first-time mother. I did this to help myself and my child, so that we both come out of it as winners. And, I sincerely hope it helps you too.

A Doctor Explains a New Mother's Most Pressing Question: When and What Should I Feed My Infant?

'The question I get asked the most by new mothers is this: When should the transition from a liquid to semi-liquid to semi-solid diet happen?

I can understand why mothers are concerned about this. It can be worrying to introduce a certain diet to a helpless new infant at the wrong time. So in this section, I will try to clarify and explain this question,' says Dr Chittal.

On Milk

All babies begin with a liquid diet, their mother's milk. Those mothers, for whom the milk may not be adequate, or the child requires more than what the mother can provide, should start with formula feeds. From here onwards, one can switch to unprocessed cow's milk. Pasteurised cow's milk can be started at six months of age. And homogenized, or tetra pack milk should only be started once the baby is a year old.

A note of caution: Buffalo's milk is a complete no-no.

The Transition

The change in a baby's diet must follow this pattern: from liquid to semi-liquid to semi-solid to solid. And the texture of food will change from pasty to grainy to lumpy to solid. The changes should be gradual as the baby's structural as well as functional maturity improves with age.

At birth: At this stage, the baby must be on a liquid, milk diet to begin with (eight feeds of milk in twenty-four hours).

1–2 months: Baby is still on a milk diet (seven feeds of milk, one feed holiday).

3 months: Start feeding your baby a little bit of rice water along with his or her milk feeds (reduce two feeds of milk).

4 months: The baby will start drooling, or begin producing a lot of saliva, which is a good indicator that the baby wants to eat food. This means that it is time to switch from liquid to semi-liquid food. The first food, of course, is to introduce rice-based cereals. Simple gravy items like plain khichdi or rice kheer will work.

5–6 months: At this stage, you can generally transition to a wheat-based diet or cereals as the baby can now digest slightly more complex food. Corn or oats milk porridge are the best foods for the baby now (at 6 months: five feeds of milk and two feeds of cereals).

7 months: You will now be introducing the philosophy of moving from unstructured food to structured food, similar to how we have whole meals (breakfast, lunch and dinner) at this stage when the baby starts accepting more solids than liquids (four feeds of milk, three feeds of cereals).

9 months: At this stage, the baby is more on solid food and less liquid (three feeds of milk, four feeds of cereals).

Foods to be avoided

Avoid all spicy, oily, refined foods like chocolates, Indian sweets, pastries, etc. All these foods have a high Glycemic Index (GI), which will make the baby hyperactive and later, lead to obesity. These foods should only be introduced much later in age or avoided altogether. Jaggery, which has a low GI, should always be used instead of white sugar.

Yellow fat, otherwise called trans fat, is fat that remains solid at room temperature (like cheese slices and cheese spread). These must be avoided too. Instead opt for good fat—fat which remains thin at room temperature—like homemade ghee.

5

Mom's the Word

Women today live in the best of times.

Never before have we entered the workplace in greater numbers nor have had the ability to earn a living from the comfort of our home. Technology and connectivity have allowed us the luxury to work within close range of our loved ones. But whether you are a working mom or a stay-at-home one, motherhood is motherhood, right? I could not write a book about children and not include a chapter on what it means to be a mother today.

Both working mothers and stay-at-home moms are faced with their own unique set of challenges. Every morning, when they leave their children behind as they head out to work, working mothers are struck by guilt; they worry that they aren't spending enough time with their kids, are missing important moments in their kids' lives and, more urgently, they worry about the safety of their children. On the other hand, stay-at-home mothers worry that their children will not be independent enough. They are also concerned about how family can sometimes take over their lives, obliterating their own personalities and desires. I've come to understand that these challenges are unique to new mothers, no matter what your situation is. And being a Scorpio, and inquisitive by nature, I wanted to know more.

I wanted to know how mothers, apart from me and my friends and family, deal with the trials and tribulations of everyday life. So I put together a survey and conducted extensive research on the results. The aim was to find out if there was a common thread that ran through all our lives—what are our challenges, our concerns and how did we tackle them? You'll find them voicing their innermost worries and concerns, with regard to motherhood and parenting, peppered throughout this chapter. I want to bring to you the stories of women who overcome hurdles daily, and are shining beacons of motherhood, whatever their circumstances.

But before we get there, I'd like to tell you the stories of two women—mothers—who shaped my life. Because as they say: first write what you know best!

~

My mother, Hema Malini, and my mother-in-law, Puja Takhtani, couldn't be more different.

One has always been a working mother, and the other, always a stay-at-home mother. My mother barely knows how to cook, while my mother-in-law cooks like a dream; the kitchen has been the centre of her life and her children say that her chicken biryani is the best in the world. My mother-in-law has always lived with her husband, cooking and packing him his tiffin for many years. While my mother lives on her own.

I have always been intrigued by how these women— both of whom play a huge role in my life—are truly a stark study in contrasts. I have seen their challenges and successes and marvelled at both their achievements. Yet, I am different. I am a hybrid. I am a working mother who can (sometimes) stay at home and still do her job. I wrote my book from my home office! So it's interesting to delve into their lives to analyse what made me the way I am today.

And I'll begin with my mother because before I assumed any other role in life, I was a daughter first and foremost.

~

From a very young age, I knew there was something different about my mother.

When we'd go out to restaurants or airports or anywhere else, people were always drawn to her. They wanted to take photographs with my mother, take her autograph or simply shake her hand. My mother also took me along to many of her shoots in Goa, Mysore and even, abroad. When I was ten months old, my parents, along with Kishore Kumar, took me on a US tour for many months. I was backstage during all the events and heard and imbibed everything. It's one of the reasons I love Kishore Kumar's music so much.

I would see her on film sets among the producers, directors and crew, and what I noticed (and loved the most) was how people reacted to her. When they'd see my mother they'd smile and beam with happiness and want to be near her. No one frowned while looking at her. And I intuitively knew that that was something good and it filled me with joy. My mother would also have frequent dance practices at home and when I visited my friends' homes their mothers wouldn't be dancing. I was convinced that she was different, but I was also confused about the whys and hows—I didn't understand that she was a celebrity and a public persona back then. I also see the same confusion and wonder in Radhya today. When I go anywhere and people take my picture, I notice that she's watching very carefully. But, just like me back then, she's not yet understood it. Only much later, when I was three-and-a-half or four years old, when I started to watch my mother's movies, did I piece it all together. And of course, later on in school, when I noticed that I was looked at and heard people whispering that I was so and so's daughter, it clicked. Don't get me wrong, I didn't like the attention. But I was beginning to understand that my mother was made of something special. And that I was the luckiest girl in the world to have her. As I grew up, she gave me an education like no school could ever give me.

My mother is the quintessential working woman. She has the strongest work ethic I've come across in a person. She started professional dance and acting at an age when most young women today are still finding their feet at college. But I don't have to tell you about her many successes. You probably already know how Hema Malini carved out her career, and what a fabulous career it is! But people don't know Hema Malini the mother. The one who dressed up her kids, told them stories to make them eat, and sometimes, also struggled with guilt and regret. There's one incident in particular that she says she can never forget.

Every evening, as a three-year-old, I would scamper over our neighbour's low boundary wall to play with the kids there. That day, it had been raining all afternoon and the garden was wet. While playing, I slipped and hit my head against a marble slab. It hurt, but I had no idea of the extent of the damage because I couldn't see for myself. Since there was a low wall between the two houses, I screamed out to my aunt, Prabha, 'Pappu!' I yelled.

She appeared at a window and when she saw my face, she gasped. 'Oh my god, Bittoo (my nickname at home)! What happened?'

Looking at her flabbergasted expression, I got worried. I touched my head and saw blood on my hands. I panicked. Suddenly, all I wanted was my mother. Immediately. But she was away on a shoot out of Bombay. Pappu rushed me to the bathroom and when I saw my face in the mirror, I thought I was going to die. One line repeated itself in my head. *'I'm going to die, and I want my mother.'* When they put me in the car, it began to pour, complete with thunder and lightning. I lay on Pappu's lap as she held a napkin to my head to stem the flow of blood. It was one of the worst car journeys of my life because what I needed was my mother, there at that very moment, and she wasn't around. I thought I was going to die without seeing her. I was distraught and a wreck. It sounds very funny now but that day, as a four-year-old, the world had truly come to an end for me.

One would dismiss this saying, 'Oh, but all children fall and get hurt.' No, not for me. That incident so profoundly affected me that years later, at a workshop conducted by my guruji, Shri Amma Bhagwan, it was revealed that I have deep-rooted issues of fear and separation from my mother. That day, when I hurt my head, had emotionally wrecked my mind for a long period of my life and it is one of the reasons why, even today, I don't like leaving my mother for too long or why I'm so attached to her. If you think I'm exaggerating, here's my mother's account to prove it.

'When they called me and told me what had happened, all I knew was that I needed to be with Esha immediately,' my mother says, who still rues that fateful day. 'I rushed back home to my daughter. Even though by then, my aunt and mother and my immediate family had already taken her to the doctor, and she was fine, my heart was heavy with guilt. Perhaps, I thought, it wouldn't have happened had I been there. Even after all these years, my heart still wrings with regret and guilt every time I see the scar [When I'd first started acting, I was known as The Girl with the Scar on her Forehead!], although it's faint, on her forehead. As a mother you can never forget and forgive yourself if your babies get hurt.

'There have been other times as a mother when I have been torn with guilt,' she continues. 'As an actress, and a public persona, there are many invites to events and parties that come my way. When my children were very young, I would dread these invites because I never liked leaving them behind, even if it was only for an hour or two.

Truth be told, I never enjoyed myself at these events because I longed to be home with my babies.

'Esha was very attached to me; she never liked to leave my side,' says my mother. 'She was always sticking to me. The first time we sent her to playschool was a big separation time for me. She was crying so much. She didn't want to go inside the classroom. And I couldn't bear to part with her too. I had tears in my eyes. Her father gently handled the situation and brought me home. She stayed for one hour and we brought her back. Initially, it was a struggle to get her to school but once she started observing the other children, she started enjoying the experience. Esha was, and still is, a stubborn person. Even as a child she had a mind of her own. If she didn't want to go somewhere, she'd lie down and become very stiff and heavy so that she couldn't be carried at all. She always wanted me to carry her and I would give in. Till she was about two or three years old, I used to carry her piggyback all the way to the second floor without the help of a lift. She was a very curious and smart baby and an extremely fast learner. She was a social child who got along with all the children who would drop by. She was also the leader of the pack; it's something I see even now—her leadership qualities. But despite all this, she was a mama's baby.

'When I would get dressed to go to a party, she would sneak up on me, ready with a cotton ball of nail polish remover, and quickly swipe away my nail polish. It was her way of keeping me behind. Of course, I would give anything to just stay home and be with her, but I also had to honour my promises and commitments. So I tried to take her wherever it was possible when I was working. When she was three years old, I took her along with me to the shoot of *Jaan Hatheli Pe*, which was happening in Goa. In the movie, Dharamji and I had a song together. It was a sad song about separation. Esha was sitting and watching the shoot, and then suddenly, she burst out crying. She was moved by the scene and nothing could stop her tears. The whole unit came to a stop to placate her. She was always overtly concerned about her mother!

'One day, Esha came back from school and asked me why I didn't cook for her like her friends' mothers. My heart fell. I felt very bad and so I rushed to the kitchen to whip up whatever I could. Truth be told, I barely knew how to make anything. My mother, who saw me in the kitchen, immediately admonished me, "The kitchen is no place for you," she said sternly. "I didn't raise you to be here." Of course, I understood my mother's good intentions but at the same time, I wanted to be a mother to my children too. I didn't want to disappoint them. And so eventually, I did learn how to cook (a little) and sometimes whisked together a few treats for my children. But all this being said, I work because I love and enjoy what I do. I can never think of sitting idle and doing nothing. In fact, my second work innings was after I had two babies. It never stopped me.'

Mother's guilt is a real thing. Millions of working mothers suffer from it every day. This is what a few women who took the survey had to say about it.

'There's always mom guilt,' says Simone Khambatta, a working mother of two babies, 'I'm always fighting the thought that I am a "bad mom" for working. And it's really hard when you have to travel; because our parents live overseas there's no immediate help, so I always turn to Google and my huge mommy network for help.'

It's only natural for a new mother to feel guilty when they are getting back to work after they've been immersed in their baby's world for so long. Being separated from your child when you first send them to school or when you have to return to work after maternity leave is a terrifying experience. At some point in her life, every working mother has been (or will be) torn with guilt, despite her successes and achievements. My mother, the iconic Hema Malini, too, has been wracked by it as you can see from her stories. She hides it from her public life, but that doesn't mean that she doesn't feel it.

But work is important. And here are some voices of true blue working moms telling it like it is.

Malaika Khan, working mother of two boys, seven and eleven years old, says, 'Everybody must work, that is how you bring in the things that you need for you and your family. Nothing comes for free.' Whether you do it out of necessity or passion, there's no getting around the fact that one day we will have to let go of our children, even it's for a few hours in a day.

'My biggest challenge as a working mom is dealing with mom guilt,' says Rinni Talwar, a mother of a two-year-old. 'We live as a single unit family with no backup. So if the nanny goes, I am home bound and that's tough as a working mom. I've come to rely on my family for help. And grandparents and siblings are a boon. But that doesn't mean I don't have fears. I worry that I won't be able to raise my child the way I would like to as I won't always have the time to dedicate towards his upbringing. I try to adjust my schedule to match my child's so I can be there at least 75 per cent of the time when he needs me.'

Then there's Priyanka Khanna, a working mother of two children, aged two and five, who says, 'My biggest fear about raising my child is their security. I'm constantly feeling guilty that I am not spending enough time with them.'

I, too, cannot imagine a life where I don't work. It goes without saying that I've inherited my work ethic from my mother. From her I learned how to value commitments, turn up on time, give my job a 100 per cent and to be kind to people. Very few people know that if it hadn't been for my mother, I may not have been in films.

'Dharamji never wanted Esha to be in films,' my mother says. 'It was almost prohibited. But I was keen that she should at least learn how to dance since it was my tradition. I took her to most of my dance practices and performances. I would place her in the make-up room, and after every performance I would rush back to her to check on her and then rush back to the stage. I will not say it was easy. As a professional, I had to maintain a fine balance between being a performer and a mother. And I wanted to do both these jobs well. But every time I rushed back, I'd be comforted to find Esha busy, happily wearing all my jewellery (which I had to wear for the next number), looking adorable. Gradually, she developed a natural interest in wearing costumes, make-up and jewellery because she saw me doing it. At movie shoots, the moment my make-up man arrived, before me, Esha would be sitting on the chair, demanding that her make-up be done first! Lipstick, blush, eye shadow—everything. Every time she'd spy my costume wigs, she had to wear it first, before me, and then prance about with it. Those moments still make me smile. Dharamji would be incensed by this. He said this would encourage her to join films—which he was firmly against—but I let her be.'

So how can a working mother manage her guilt and still do a good job at work? I found the answer during my research for this book.

'I am a director of a company with vast responsibilities. I love working; it keeps my mind alive,' says Natasha Jitender Irani, a working mother of a ten-month-old baby. 'The biggest challenge for me is not being around the baby when I am at work. My most valued tools to help me cope are reliable staff and a few close friends and family who have had kids, and whom I trust, who have helped me a lot when it comes to raising my child. My baby is young, so I don't have any specific fears, because I wake up with the baby and she comes to visit me at work in the middle of the day and I put her to bed. But I can't stop wondering if she misses me or if she is okay. I used to micromanage but after the baby, I had to learn how to delegate and prioritize, which I learnt are crucial when you're a working mom.'

Prioritizing is key. From my mother, I've learnt how to work and also find a balance in my personal life. When Radhya was born, I took time off and focused on my first born. I was very clear that I didn't want to take off for months to a faraway destination for a shoot and leave my daughter behind. Today I'm at a stage where I choose the work that suits my lifestyle; and I choose quality over quantity. I only work on projects that are both satisfying and logistically doable. The work I do now is not very time consuming but it's also creatively satisfying. I don't settle for work that I don't believe in or enjoy. I think one of the most important pieces of advice for a new working mother is prioritizing and finding balance. If you are a working mother reading this, take some time to think about this. It will unlock a world of peace and contentment once you can strike the right balance. Remember, balance is about both striking a compromise and feeling satisfied.

'I used to worry that I would miss spending time with them, hampering their development. And that no one would be able to look out for my kids like I do. I feared leaving them with other support systems like nannies, family, etc.,' says Aparna Shah, a mother of twins, 'Today, I have just started work on a flexible basis so I can balance work and caring for my family. But I do take help from my family.'

Children of working parents can sometimes feel like they've been abandoned. They may long for their parents, like I once did briefly, feelings like 'I wish my mother (or father) was here with me', or 'she took me to classes' or a hundred other things. This can get aggravated if they see mothers of other children spending more time with them. So, as a mother, when you notice that your child is beginning to understand and figure things out for themselves, it is very important to explain to your child and make them understand why you work. That you work *not* because you want to be away from them, or that you don't love them, or you don't want to spend time with them. If you're not clear on these points, your child will start inventing their own stories and may just begin to resent you. You need to be open and clear and explain things to them in a friendly way: 'Mama needs to go. Mama needs to work because she needs to earn money, which will buy XYZ.' Engage and explain to your child the benefits of working. This usually does the job.

That being said, there will come some important emotional moments, events and milestones in every child's life when they need their parent. It could be anything, from the first time they failed, or won, or got caught doing something bad, got hurt, was bullied, etc. Your child will have her own unique moments and it's your job to be there for them when they need you. For example, when I was in class nine, I once came back home in a frightful state. I had cheated in my biology exam and had gotten caught. The school was going to suspend me for the year. When I got home, the living room was full of people, and it was the last place I wanted to be. All I knew was that I needed to tell my mother, but she wasn't there. So I went up to her room and locked myself in. When my mother returned and found me there, I spilled my guts. Of course, she gave me a piece of her mind for cheating, but I had never felt better nor more relieved than when I saw and confided in her.

Children need emotional support and strength from their mothers. Working mothers should also try to dedicate Sundays (or any other day during which they are free) to spend time with their child. Taking the child on a holiday, to the park, a movie or an event can be a great way to bond with them and show them that you are theirs.

Now we come to the bedrock of what enables and allows a working mother to excel at work, worry-free. The pillar and foundation that will enable you to do what you do well is *family*. The best support system that you can ever have as a working mom is your family. They are the people who you can trust, are responsible and will have your back when you need them.

'My in-laws are my biggest support in raising my son,' says working mom, Rhea Gursahani, a mother of a two-year-old. 'If I can work in peace for seven hours a day it's only because I know there is family looking after my child. Even with all the help you have, the sense of stability and peace comes only on knowing that there is somebody to count on from within the immediate family.'

My mother could go out into the world and dazzle everyone with her talent because she has a rock-solid foundation. 'My mother, Jaya Chakraverty, my aunt, my family were my biggest support systems when I was working or had to leave my children for work,' she says. 'My mother kept a hawk eye on the babies. And if she wasn't there, then it was my aunt. Aunts are like second mothers. My aunt supported me through my career, travelling with me everywhere, on shoots and events. Without my family, I would never have been able to leave my children without worrying all the time, and I wouldn't have been able to do a good job.'

This brings me to my mother-in-law—Puja Takhtani—whose care epitomizes the importance of family and selfless love. Once, many years ago, her happiness lay in the kitchen. For her, feeding her family was how she communicated her love for them. Today, with the help of my sister-in-law, Astha, she has finally handed over the kitchen to others and taken up her other interests and hobbies. But since I lived with her for a long time, I have seen both aspects of her life. While I can see that she's changed to become more independent, she's taught me the values of family and how to care for your loved ones. Her story can't be more different from my mother's, but it will find resonance with women who are stay-at-home mothers.

'I had been brought up in a joint family and was married when I was eighteen,' says Puja Takhtani. 'Although very dominant, my mother-in-law, Vidya Takhtani, was a loving soul. For example, sometimes she would take us shopping and decide what was best for us! She had a very big heart and was filled with generosity. Of course, there were times when she'd sharply point out my mistakes. And back then, as a new bride in a new family, I would be hurt by what she said. Only much later, I realized that even though she was tough on me, she'd always had my best interests at heart. She sacrificed her whole life so that her children got the best in life; she was very strict with them. Even when she was in her fifties, she would wake up at the crack of dawn and cook for the entire family. And today, her sons are successful because of their mother. The one thing I learnt from her is that there is strength in unity and family is above all.

'And so, when it was my time to take the lead in the family, I took up the baton to carry her flame forward,' she says. 'I was passionate about cooking and the kitchen became my domain. I was a hands-on mother who changed nappies, washed her babies, cooked and fed them, told them stories every night and could be there for every happy and sad moment of theirs. In time, I became their friend. Of course, being a stay-at-home mother has its perks. I had the luxury to spend quality time with my children and my husband.

I had the luxury to watch them at close quarters and be there for them through their ups and downs in school and college. My children are humble, well-mannered, affectionate and excelled at their studies and at life. And I felt I had a role to play in it. It was very fulfilling.

'Of course, there are some drawbacks. I wasn't very confident as a person,' she says. 'It may sound strange to you, but I had never travelled, even short distances, on my own before I got married. But a woman cannot always be chaperoned about! My parents used to live in Cuffe Parade and I had never been anywhere without them. After getting married, my mother-in-law taught me how to travel by train. She would accompany me, teaching me how to buy a ticket from the station near her home to Churchgate, and from there, in a taxi to my parents' house. She would go back on her own. She was a rock-star like that. She did this exercise with me a couple of times till I was confident enough to do it on my own. Thanks to her training, today I can go anywhere on my own.

'By Shri Paramjyoti Amma Bhagwan's grace, I am truly blessed that my sons have married wonderful women. Even though Esha comes from the glitz and glamour of Bollywood, she is humble, simple and grounded with a solid value system, which she's no doubt inherited from her wonderful parents. I share a great bond with her, and she and my son are there with us through thick and thin.'

My mother-in-law grew up and lived all her life in a joint family. While it is great for raising children with the help of a populous support system which comes with the guaranteed safety for children, it can also have its drawbacks.

'I just moved out of our joint family setup. The biggest challenge was to raise my child the way I would like to,' says Vanita Dalal, mother of a five-year-old. 'There were too many opinions and different styles of how to raise a child. This would confuse my child, who would then take advantage of it! I must say though, it made me more patient!'

'The challenge of raising a child in a joint family is that everyone's opinions and methods of raising a child is very different,' says Nidhi Khanna, mother of a two-year-old. 'Getting your views across to everyone in a nice way is tricky.'

'Everyone has a different opinion!' says Akanksha Arora, working mom of a four-year-old. 'And the grandparents spoil the kids, in turn, the kids take their grandparents for granted.'

As they say, too many cooks spoil the broth!

There is one major aspect which affects many stay-at-home mothers, they forget about themselves. They stop caring about their physical and mental health and begin to focus only on their family. Think about what you are told on an airline as you're about to take off—put on your own oxygen mask first, before you put on your child's. In other words, help yourself before you help others. Because if you're not in perfect shape what good can you do for others?

To mothers who stay at home, I offer you only one piece of advice: besides the husband, the children and then, other wives or husbands, there is another person you must never forget nor take for granted—that person is *you*. You must never forget yourself amidst the daily grind and selfless care for your loved ones. Look after yourself, enrich your inner life, set aside time for yourself, develop and nurture passions and hobbies, have a set of friends who will always have your back, and take yourself out of the house.

'As a working mother, one has to be organized and plan everything in advance, if not, it definitely affects the work and daily schedule, which creates nothing but inconvenience and stress,' says Neha Joshi, a working mother of a two-year-old. 'When I am at work, I trust my family with my son. Sometimes it's very difficult to strike a balance between personal and professional lives. Because I work, I push myself harder at home, giving that much extra so that my baby doesn't feel neglected or that I don't understand his needs. But I also take time off for myself and give myself some "Me Time". I feel that it's very important for the mother to be happy; only then she can spread more happiness around. She should be able to detach herself, without feeling guilty, for a short while to take care of her needs because an overdose of anything can only cause imbalance, which is neither good for raising a child nor for living a happy life. It can be tricky to maintain this emotional balance.'

My mother-in-law, for whom the home and family were the axis of her life for many years, has finally found time for herself. I can see the change in her, and she looks positively radiant.

'Today, all my children are married and have lives of their own,' says Puja Takhtani. 'I have all the time to myself. What do I do with it? My husband and I have a set routine. We spend a lot of time together and with our lovely grandchildren. We go for daily walks to Joggers Park, and I go to the gym every day, which keeps me truly motivated. And it's great that I've also made some friends there with whom I have regular get-togethers. It's refreshing to make new friends with whom you have shared interests. When you're a stay-at-home mother, there will be people who will judge you and compare you to a working woman. Remember that there will always be people who judge, no matter what you do. But life is about learning. And you should take the opportunity to find what you love and cherish doing. I found that in spirituality.

'Six years ago, my elder son, Bharat, introduced me and my husband, Vijay, to our Guruji. He is located an hour's drive away from Chennai. I was amazed by the experience. It completely changed me. Today, we go there every month to attend sessions and pray. It's taught me that to receive we must first give, and that gratitude is the hallmark of spirituality.'

~

Motherhood and parenting are constant balancing acts—when to give and when to take, when to focus on your child and when to focus on yourself. It is something you get good at with experience and time. When I had my first baby, I was certain that I was going to give motherhood my 100 per cent, much like I did for my career. My priorities were very clear. Like my mother, I too had started working early, at eighteen, and even before that I had been dancing professionally. I've dedicated a huge chunk of my early life to movies. I wanted to give motherhood that same commitment.

Today, I think I've become good at balancing both work and my personal life. I am always working: on my production company, my books, my dance, yet I'm always there for my children. I am there to feed them, pick them up from school and take them to doctor's appointments. I don't want to miss out on their big moments. I manage to do this because I'm a meticulous planner by nature.

I research and plan my children's monthly food menus, their playtimes and their social activities down to the T. I am organized and pro-active. So I am always on the ball. Just like my work, I do it because it brings me joy and makes me happy. You don't have to be like me, but being prepared will help you in the long run. In this book, I have shown you many ways you can simplify some of the difficulties of being a new mother, and I hope that they work for you like they have worked for me.

If there's one thing I've learned as a parent, it's that there's a very thin line between obsession and neglect. Often, I tend to sway towards obsessing over my children—I have a natural tendency to micromanage and be hands-on. But when I observe myself doing so, I remind myself of my mother. Being a star, you can sometimes be wary of sending your children unaccompanied or to places you are unfamiliar with. My mother has always trusted us and given us the freedom to experience things in life, even when we were just kids. If we went wrong, she'd reprimand us, but she always allowed us to make those mistakes, and then learn from them. As a kid, I remember very few 'don'ts' in her vocabulary. She didn't obsess, wasn't paranoid or a helicopter parent. She gave us the dignity of our own individuality and lives. She gave us the gift of trust, and we returned that trust back to her, intact. And her unwavering trust in me, as a human being, is what's made me who I am.

Today, I am trying to apply this beautiful learning with my daughters. I want them to have the freedom that I had, I want them to be out in nature, playing, making friends, I want them to blossom into two lovely individuals with strong heads on their shoulders and, most importantly, I want them to be happy. And I'd like to thank my mother for being the mother every mother dreams of being.

6

Baby Boo-boos

All mother's love to be adventurous and just like the same, I too, did something bold a few years ago.

I took my seven-month-old daughter, Radhya, along with me on a trip to Los Angeles. It was her first international flight and her first major haul across continents. I was very excited about it. It was a solo trip and I was solely responsible for Radhya. The flight to LA is a long flight; with a halt in Abu Dhabi, our journey must not have been less than twenty-two hours in total. But I was feeling confident about having things in control.

Just as I boarded the flight, my baby started to feel uneasy and developed a bad stomach. And by the time the flight took off, Radhya's situation turned into full-blown tummy trouble! It was a case of loose motions, and there was no remedy at hand. I had to take full control of the situation. Throughout the flight, I was kept busy changing diapers, trying to soothe her and help her find some relief.

When we finally landed in LA I felt a sense of achievement because I had handled a crisis on my own, and it had been a difficult one—I had to cope with the knowledge that my baby had to suffer so much. But I thought my troubles had come to an end when I reached the apartment; usually, a tummy upset in babies gets sorted out quickly. However, little did I know that it had only just begun. The whole month we were in LA, Radhya suffered terrible tummy trouble. She had one of the worst stomach issues I've ever seen with her.

To make matters worse, things aren't as straightforward in America. Medical establishments are very particular about paperwork, documents have to be in place before the possibility of even showing your baby is considered by a simple nursing home. The way doctors function in the US is very different from how things are done here, in India. And this includes the medicines that they prescribe. I am very much a champion of our Indian medicines, which I feel are straightforward and fuss-free. The doctors there gave Radhya probiotic powders and made her undergo many tests, one of them being a test for lactose intolerance (from my stories you know that both my babies love milk and guzzle it in an instant)! And none of it worked because they weren't effective; the doctors were reluctant to prescribe her something stronger. It's safe to say I made many trips to the UCLA hospital, which wasn't a very good detour. And then, much later, I found out that there's a medicine—a little tube called Entrogenia—that one can find only in India, which does the trick in a jiffy. If only I'd packed it in my suitcase, it would've saved me and Radhya a world of trouble.

Today, wherever I travel, even if it's just for one day, I never leave home without a bunch of trusted and effective medicines. One box for Radhya, and another for Miraya because they are of different age groups and need different medicines and dosages.

With an infant or a toddler you never know when they can come down with an illness and what has caused it. This was the biggest lesson I learnt as a new mom. I understood that I needed to plan, not just my children's diet, but also be highly organized when it comes to their medicines and accessories. You must keep an emergency medical kit at hand at all times.

In this chapter, I want to tell you ways how you, too, can be prepared for when your baby falls ill and how to spot signs of illness before they grow into something serious. Along with my paediatrician, Dr Chittal, we tackle some of the most common baby afflictions and tell you how to solve them. But first of all, let's talk about how you can tell if your baby is under the weather.

'Babies react differently in different situations,' says Dr Chittal. 'The first few things that may happen if a baby is unwell is that the baby might stop eating, become cranky, lethargic, or they may be feverish, nauseous or pass less urine. There is no one symptom to detect what illness the baby is going through. So it is up to the mother to be watchful and report to a doctor immediately if any of the above happens.'

And as a mother I know the signs of my babies' discomfort.

The first symptom that my babies are unwell is that they begin crying relentlessly. Since an infant cannot speak, the only way he or she can tell you that they are uncomfortable or something's going on with them is by communicating through wails and tears. They get cranky because they are uneasy. This is always the first indicator for me. I then know that something's going on with them. This is my go-to sign. Not eating is secondary because many babies are fussy when it comes to food. If this is the case, I check their temperature and immediately call my paediatrician.

The most common illness that strikes babies have to do with their stomach.

Our last monsoon was a troublesome one. Our neighbourhood streets were badly waterlogged, and this eventually led to water contamination in our home. One after the other, both my girls kept coming down with bad stomachs, which led to frequent visits to the doctor, and numerous stool tests to check for stomach infections (I don't think I've ever done so many stool tests in my entire life!). Bad water means bad tummies. It was a continuous cycle: Radhya would become better, and then, Miraya would fall ill. If your babies are suffering from bad tummies, get their stool tests done and then your paediatrician will advise you thereafter.

One thing I've noticed about my babies is that if the problem is stomach related then you've got to check their tummies. Baby tummies are usually soft, but if there's a stomach-related illness then my babies' tummies become very hard. And I know then that they're usually suffering from gas issues or colic. But I'm no doctor, so here's Dr Chittal, explaining how a baby's digestion works and what you should be looking out for as a mother.

Understanding Your Baby's Digestive Health

Most babies, when they are born and soon thereafter, pass stools after every feeding. A baby is known to pass eight to ten large stools and eight to ten small stools every time the baby passes gas. Ultimately, a baby passes fifteen to twenty stools a day. These stools are not foul smelling, they may be watery and golden yellow in colour. This is a normal stool pattern.

After 1 to 1.5 months of age, a baby learns to digest milk better and they become more and more constipated; in that sense, the baby passes stools less frequently. Around the same time, the baby becomes slightly colic, which is where the baby is unable to pass gas, either from above or from below.

An important thing to be aware of is that a baby who is started off with formula and later given cow's milk may become constipated, which means they will pass hard stools. While the stools of a breastfed baby still remain soft.

Babies who are bottle-fed or have the habit of putting things in their mouth are also prone to stomach infections.

When the baby has a stomach infection, the stool pattern changes again, due to diarrhoea, which is characterized by green, watery, foul-smelling stools, and very rarely might even pass blood in the stool. Sometimes, fever and vomiting also accompany these symptoms.

Babies become colicky from 1 to 1.5 months of age, when their stool frequency reduces. When this happens, usually in the evenings, babies start crying. The baby will stretch their legs and arch their back in an attempt to force the gas out.

Therefore, observing your baby's stool is key to understanding what goes in their little tummy!

The next common illness is usually fever, but fever in itself is never the problem. Fever is always an indication that something else is off inside your baby's system. It is a symptom and must be treated accordingly.

'Fever is obvious. Babies feel warm on the head, the palms and legs,' says Dr Chittal. 'If the fever is because of infection then the baby will be fussy about eating and be very cranky. Fever has to have a reason. Either it's an external source, or more commonly, it occurs post vaccination. You can identify the source of the infection by observing if the baby is crying before passing urine, or touching the ear and crying, or having loose motion.'

If your baby is suffering from fever, I will urge you to reach out to your doctor immediately. This is not the time for home remedies.

All of this may sound dismal, but please don't give in to despair. Illness is a natural part of your baby's growth. As their body adapts, evolves and grows its resistance to external elements, they will grow stronger and more resilient. It's part and parcel of bringing up a baby. However, that being said, there are times when you can be cautious, take matters into your hands and avert more problems.

A cold is always visible, so it is the easiest to detect. Now that Radhya is going to playschool, she is exposed to many more elements than when she was at home all the time. Kids pass on colds very quickly when they start going to school, and especially in the case of those who have siblings, they bring the colds home. If one of them has a cold, it's only a matter of time before all the other kids are sneezing, coughing and sporting runny noses. When one of my babies has a cold, the other one invariably gets it. Both *will* have a cold at the same time. There are no two ways about this. This used to happen to my sister and myself when we were kids. And so, when Ahana's son and Radhya started going to school, they began to pick up minor colds, and giving it to each other. Now, Miraya is also bearing the brunt of it! It's safe to say colds trend faster than the most popular hashtag!

When Radhya first started picking up colds at playschool and passing it on to her baby sister, I was at a loss till I spoke to Dr Chittal, who gave me the most helpful tip a mother can receive. He told me to give them the flu shot.

The flu shot is heaven-sent. Not only does it keep colds at bay, but it also allows you to be stress-free during that time about your baby catching the dreaded cold and passing it on to her siblings. I suggest all mothers read up about it and consult their paediatricians and consider giving it to their children. If you're travelling, or if your child is in playschool, or it's the time of the year when most people fall sick, especially during the monsoons, the flu shot is an absolute life saver and a must.

In fact, another important preventative measure is to vaccinate your children on time. As you already know how organized and OCD I can be, I maintain a file for both my daughters and set reminders on my calendar for their vaccination due dates. That way I'll never miss a thing!

Some baby problems new parents just cannot escape confronting. And that's teething. All babies will grow their teeth at some point, even if they don't fall ill. Teething is going to be a part of your life for the first year or year-and-a-half, depending on how quickly your baby gets their teeth. With me, the first experience with teething was what my mother and mother-in-law told me: '*Jab bacche ka pet kharab hote hai*, then they are getting their teeth (When a baby suffers from an upset stomach he or she is generally teething).' But as a parent we must be observant. When a baby gets loose motion, we are inclined to think that it's a normal tummy upset, but more often than not, it's related to teething. If the stomach issues continue for a long time without resolution, it's usually this. Fever is another symptom of teething. And of course, it's also the case when they aren't eating their food. When they have a fever the child becomes even more cranky because teething is generally already quite painful; it's a double whammy for them. Radhya started getting her teeth quite early, before she was one, and then she stopped eating.

So, what do you do when they are teething? I went back to feeding Radhya liquid and mashed food. I fed her a lot of curd rice and banana (this also helps stop loose motions, and it worked for me when I was a kid). I gave her a lot of liquids and soups, and of course, milk, which is a saviour. And the proportion should always be half milk, half water—never whole milk.

As parents, you must keep your eyes on your baby and see them as a whole, instead of isolating one single symptom and treating it. It is a complicated time for our little ones because they are gradually being exposed to the big bad world for the first time, and it's only been a few days since they've arrived into this world, and in that time, they're experiencing an assault on their system and senses. It doesn't help that they can't communicate with us through words, but if you look closely, they are telling us everything we need to know through their body language and sleep, food and poop patterns.

So that's the bulk of baby troubles, however, there are a few more pointers I'd like to share with you about daily life with your babies. This is something I myself had the most questions about as a new mother and it was related to travel. How do I travel with babies? What do I pack? And, what do I do in emergency situations? Of course, now that I have two babies, I'm much wiser, even though every day is a learning process. There are a few things I've learnt in my journey and I think these can come to your rescue as a new mother who has to travel.

Travel, today, is an inevitable part of our lives. Whether it's for holiday or for work, most people today will need to travel, with or without their babies. Travelling with babies is such fun because it gives you the opportunity to make beautiful memories with them. That being said, little babies are also susceptible to illnesses, especially when they are out of their comfort zone.

My number one suggestion when you are travelling with babies is to be super organized. A little planning and wracking your brains before you travel will always reward you with a stress-free journey, your baby and your ease and, of course, a great holiday!

The first and most important rule of travelling with children is to always, always, keep a copy of your baby's medical files with you. These days, when I'm travelling, I take a Xerox copy of both my babies' files—which include all their prescriptions—with me, and I carry all the medicines; that way, I don't have to run helter-skelter at the last moment. I keep a copy of these files in my daughters' luggage too. So that I always have everything handy. It's much easier this way.

And when I'm travelling abroad, I write down all the alternative medicines to our Indian counterparts because you may not find those particular medicines in a foreign country. It's good to have the information at hand rather than scrambling for it in the last minute. I told you I learnt a heavy lesson after my LA fiasco! Call me crazy, but I'd rather be safe than sorry!

Next, we come to what to feed the baby while travelling. Feeding your baby on your travels is also another challenge.

I believe that you should always feed your baby home-cooked food when you can, especially when they are much too young to be able to digest new ingredients. For example, I always feed home-cooked food to Miraya when we are travelling. So whether it's a hotel room or a place abroad to stay for a while, I carry a little pantry set with me wherever I go when I'm with my kids! This includes packets of rice, dal, Indian masalas, and so on. I pack these in Ziplock packets and label them properly. And the magnum opus of this improvised travelling pantry is this really cool, heaven-sent, Japanese cooker from the brand, Yazawa, which folds into the size of a compact disk, and can easily be packed. The cooker also has a convenient dish inside it, which is super handy to use. And since it's an electric cooker, all I have to do is plug it in and I'm good to go!

Of course, I don't carry the vegetables with me! I haven't lost it completely! What I do is I locally source the veggies and find out where to get local eggs and cow's milk. Mostly, I figure out this information before I reach my destination by asking locals, or friends who live there or by researching it on the Net. If things like pulses, rice and masalas are easily available, then I don't bother carrying them. I don't want to be one of those Indians whose bags are opened at security checks to find bottles of pickles and curd, which then have to be thrown away. Although, truth be told, something similar has happened to me and my mother years ago!

The other great tip I can give you when you are travelling with your kids is to choose a service apartment rather than a hotel. It's one of the best decisions a parent can make when travelling with children. In fact, even before we became parents, Bharat and I have always preferred service apartments. We always avoid hotels because they are too restrictive for the kids. I prefer service apartments because they are usually more spacious, allow you the freedom to cook meals for your kids, have room enough for the kids to play and run around and you can open the windows and let fresh air in—unlike most hotels, which are centrally air conditioned. You can make it feel like home.

My diaper bag is also home to many baby essentials. A well-organized diaper bag can also save you a lot of trouble and last-minute scurrying around for things. Since I am particular about these things, I ensure that the diaper bag I carry always includes diapers of course, but also baby mats, rash creams, water wipes, disposable packets for throwing diapers, a couple of SOS medicines, a couple of packets of snacks, some fruit, flasks with normal and hot water and milk, a few change of clothes for the babies and a light blanket. Things that I also find useful and always carry with me are see-through Ziplock bags to section things neatly. It's easy to pull things up in an emergency. Water wipes are great because they are made of 99.9 per cent water and are super gentle for your baby. You can order these online. One of the most amazing accessories to have at hand are flavoured straws. They come in many flavours—chocolate, strawberry, banana—and are great for days when your baby is being fussy about drinking their milk.

So there you have it—all my tips, advice and crazy planning techniques. I hope these come in handy for you if you are ever in a quandary about your baby's health. But most of all, I pray that you are in the first place.

7

Big Baby, Flip-Out Mummy

How time flies! It was only just yesterday when I'd started writing this book and now, we're already at the final chapter. I hope you've enjoyed reading it as much as I did writing it; I hope that this book has helped you through your entry into motherhood. But before you leave, I am reminded about another moment in my life when time felt like it had flown, right through my grasp and much more quickly than I'd realized. It's something all new mothers experience at a certain stage and I'd like to share my experience with you. After all, the phrase 'separation anxiety' is one that a mother dreads the most.

If I had a magic potion that would stop all our babies from growing up, I'd use it in a heartbeat. But that's impossible. We mothers must sigh and throw up our hands as we watch time work its power over our babies. From crawling, to taking their first step, to saying their first word and eating solid food, every tiny moment is a special landmark in a mother's heart. But not the day when I had to send Radhya to playschool. No, no—that was the worst day in my whole life!

But before she went to playschool, Radhya and I did many months of Mother Toddlers, a kind of preparation ground, till she was eligible to go to playschool. Mother Toddlers is great because you can be with your baby, watch them fool around, play and develop curiosities about objects and things. It's a lovely bonding exercise, and I suggest that every mother do it if they have the time. I really enjoyed my experience there. After this, we had a two-month holiday—with no school. This also coincided with the time when I was due to have my second baby. So you can blame the hormones or the fact that I'd spent two unbroken months wrapped up in baby world, but suddenly, I became aware that this lovely period was swiftly coming to an end. I had to send Radhya to playschool and there was no getting around it. That's when I snapped.

It's safe to say I'm a cautious and vigilant personality. But when it comes to my children, this aspect of my personality hits another level of crazy! For example, my husband sometimes likes to take Radhya on morning drives, before he goes off to work. And even though I know she's with her dad (and cannot be safer), I can never relax till she is back under my gaze! Then there are times when Bharat wants to take her to visit cousins and friends for playdates and so on, and guess what? I'm always there. *I'm just always there*! I would never let my babies out of my sight if I could manage it. I'm just not ready for it yet (and I don't think I'll ever be!). That's how crazy I am! So the thought of leaving my first born, even if it was only for two hours at playschool, officially made me flip out with bouts of anxiety.

I spent many nights awake, imagining scenarios that could go wrong: Radhya crying and hating school, her thinking that I was sending her away alone because there was a new baby in the house. By day, I would turn into one indecisive ping-pong ball who'd call the school and the principal to tell them that I actually wouldn't be sending Radhya that year after all, that she could continue with Mother Toddlers, which we actually did for a session or two, but Radhya was so disinterested, she did not even look at the babies because they were not her age. She had grown out of toddler world and here I was, trying to make her do it all over again.

At other times, I'd tell my mother that we could get tutors home to teach her till she turned three-and-a-half years old. I mean, why did such a small baby need to go to school anyway?! I am not someone who expresses my emotions too easily, but for two months before playschool,

I was not in a happy place deep inside. I became a woman obsessed and drove everyone at home up the wall.

Finally, my mother sat me down and told me that I had to stop panicking. That she, too, had sent both her daughters, Ahana and me, to school and had cried desperately the first time. That I was going to be okay in about a week and would begin to enjoy it. And that I had to give Radhya a chance to make friends, socialize and enjoy the process of learning and growing up. I had to give her a chance.

And I did, of course.

A month after school had already started!

And only once the principal called me and asked me to.

So the dreaded day finally came. While Radhya went off to class, I sat outside the whole time (the principal and teachers were kind enough to let me), doing not much except stressing that she would come running out, crying, looking for her Mama. And guess what? She did none of that. Save for a few initial tears, she was fine.

I give complete credit to the principal and teachers of the school as to how they handled me, my mood swings and indecisiveness for a whole month—anyone else would've told me to find a new school and get out! My mother and my husband also played a huge role in keeping me sane through all this crazy! Their balancing and cool Libran values were like a bucket of ice-cold water on this hot, brooding Scorpion.

Now, Radhya's comfortable and happy. But sending her to playschool was one of the toughest things I've had to do. Sending her to the bigger school will be another emotional roller-coaster, but I know that I'll be better equipped to handle it. I'm still giving my family enough notice so they're prepared for another round of crazy.

But also, now that Radhya is in playschool (and in a matter of time Miraya will also be off), I have the time to take up more demanding projects. I've seen many women (my mother is a good example of this) experience a second gust of wind in their careers once their babies are at school. I look forward to working guilt-free, taking up the threads, once they've grown up a little. And if I have to travel internationally for a longer duration, then there's no doubt that I'd take my babies along! Of course, that's when they're in junior school. Till they are of a responsible age, I'm not taking any chances.

With school comes the business of tiffin. Already I've begun thinking and planning about how to keep their tiffins interesting and keep them motivated to be healthy. Children's tastes change ever so quickly, and it's really just a matter of catching up and staying clued in. I recently noticed that Radhya, who enjoyed eating Indian, suddenly didn't want to eat it anymore. She had gotten bored of it.

So I had to change my entire food plan to adapt to her palate. Now she's eating more continental fare and is enjoying it while she does. Planning your child's tiffins is a constant tug of war between what you think your child *wants* to eat versus what you think they *should* be eating. It will require constant change, innovation, adaption and upgradations to their preferences.

My Easy Tips to Planning Your Child's Tiffin

I have three rules of keeping your children's tiffin boxes fun and nutritious.

The first is you need to observe your child and see what they're enjoying; my first rule of feeding your babies, which we've talked about in depth earlier in the book.

The second rule: home-cooked is better than any other kind of food. Choose home-cooked food over pre-packaged, packet or store bought items any day.

And the final rule: variety. Today, when I pack my daughter's tiffin, I give her two or three different snacks in smaller quantities, rather than a lot of one thing. So, for example, I pack her a makhana, a small sandwich and some cut fruit. This way her

My He-Man, my superhero! With Papa in our farmhouse when I was two-and-a-half years old

Copy cat! Three-year-old me on Mamma's lap, twinning in kaftans

With my love (Bharat) on our babymoon in Greece

Spending some precious time with Bharat (I am carrying Radhya)

Radhya's first photo shoot at three months by Subi Samuel

With my Radhya Bome ('doll' in Tamil)

With my Miu (Miraya)

Miu bonding with her Dadaa
(Bharat)

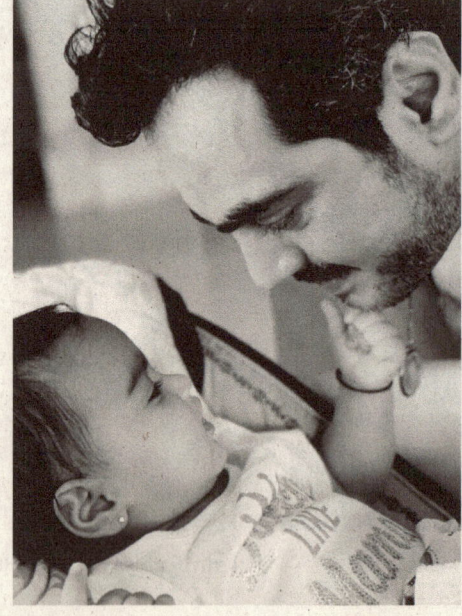

Ten-day-old Miraya's naming ceremony with my parents, Bharat and both the baby girls (Miraya on my lap and Radhya on Bharat's)

The Takhtanis (From L to R: Me, Bharat, Radhya, Vijayji—my father-in-law, Pujaji—my mother-in-law, Devesh and Astha (Bharat's brother and his wife) in Bahrain for a family wedding, where I am expecting Miraya (five months pregnant)

Me and my mini-me doing something we both love—cuddling!

BFFs for life! The protective big sister, Radhya, has baby sister, Miraya, on her lap

Noodles time! Radhya enjoying dinner on her high chair

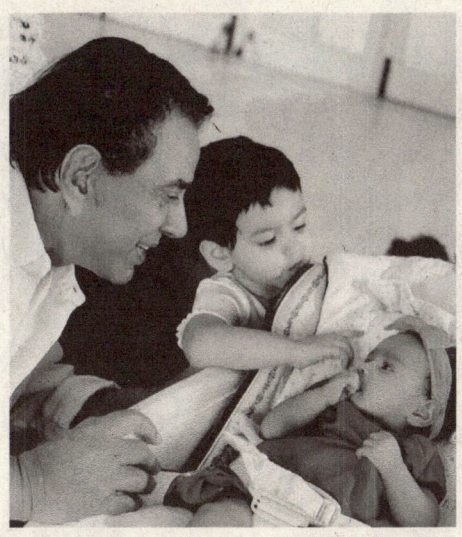

A special moment with Nanu! Radhya stands near
Dharamji as they watch over two-month-old Miraya

Two peas in a pod! Radhya with her Nanu

Radhya and Miraya with Nani Maa
(don't miss Radhya's lipstick)

Welcoming Miraya home

tiffin remains interesting and she won't get bored eating just one thing. If your child doesn't want to eat one thing, she or he still has two more things to reach out for.

And that's it—all my stories, my fears, my joys and my advice. I hope I've helped arm you with useful tips and tricks, planners and recipes that will enrich your motherhood. And that you're richer for this experience. Motherhood can make us do crazy things—I started writing this book while I was pregnant! And so, I hope this book in turn, inspires you to take up that idea you've perhaps been nursing or toying with and help make it a reality. There's never a better time to do something challenging and interesting than when you're a mother!

But before I sign off, there's one small and final piece of advice I'd like to share with all new mothers. In our chaotic and beautiful journey of motherhood, we can tend to sometimes forget or leave out an essential person in our family: the husband. And it's normal to do so when we're so focused on making sure that our babies are perfectly okay. But the strength of parenting lies in the strength of a family. It's very important to keep your husband happy. After all, none of this would have happened without him! After my second baby, for a short while, I noticed that Bharat was cranky and irritated with me. He felt that I wasn't giving him enough attention. It is very natural for a husband to feel this way because at that time, I was *consumed* with Radhya's playschool fiasco and feeding Miraya, and I was also between writing my book and dealing with my production meetings. So, he felt neglected. And I immediately noticed the error of my ways. I remembered the times when Bharat had asked me for a new toothbrush, and it had slipped my mind, or when his shirts hadn't been pressed or when I sent him off to work without bothering to check what he'd been given for lunch. He's a man of very few needs, and if I couldn't look after him, there was something wrong. I quickly made sure to rectify it. Bharat is different; he tells me directly, to my face, if he senses a problem. But there may be men who are not so forthcoming. It falls on you to keep the romance alive. I figured that I hadn't gone out for date nights or a movie with him in a while. So I decided to step out of my tracks, loosen my bun, wear a nice dress and go out with him on the weekends.

Spend time with your husband, remind him of the woman he's fallen in love with and that he too is part of the journey. Between your work and your children, try to find the time to pamper and care for him too. You need his support just as much as he needs yours.

~

As parents we all have big dreams for our children. I don't dream that my daughters will grow up to be actresses, nor is my husband dreaming that they will grow up to join him in the jewellery business. They will learn for themselves and figure out where their interests lie. Tomorrow, if my daughters want to become police commissioners or lawyers, it's their choice. They can choose their boyfriends, husbands, clothes, lifestyles—everything. But there is something I definitely want for them—and that is they strive to be achievers like all the women in their family. Be it my grandmother, my aunt, my mother or even me, we're all strong women who've had the balls to do things our way. We've always worked hard and stood our ground. We don't get swayed by external forces. And I want my daughters to be like that. I want them to be respectful of elders, which I see lacking today, and like me, I want them to be proud Indians.

And if I have to remind them of something along the way, it'll be this small but potent word: dignity. It's very important for women to be dignified. You can be bold, loud, wear what you want, there's nothing wrong with all that—but women with grace and dignity stand out, and that's what I want for my daughters. I want them to stand on their own two feet, chin up, looking the world in the eye. Imagine my happiness when recently,

I received a text message from Radhya's teacher, who wrote: 'Your daughter is not one to get bullied, she'll give it back!'

That's my girl!

RECIPES FOR BABIES

AMMA MIA'S CUCINA

For Babies between 6 Months to 1 Year

BREAKFAST OR SNACKS

1. Countryside Oats and Apple Porridge

Ingredients
1 apple
1 almond (badam)
2 dates (khajur)
¼ cup oats

Directions
- Peel the skin of the apple and grate it till you get 2 tbsp. of grated apple. Grate the almond as well.
- Chop the dates finely.
- In a pan, boil 1–1.5 cups of water.

- Add the oats, grated apple, almond and dates. Stir well. Let it cook for 8–10 minutes and keep stirring at regular intervals.
- Let it cool and serve.

2. Soothing Baked Apple with Rice

Ingredients
1 apple
4 tbsp. rice cereal
Breast milk or formula

Directions
- After removing the seeds, put the apple in a baking pan and add a little water. Cook the apple until it is tender.
- Mix cereal and milk.
- Remove the skin of the apple and blend it, separately.
- Add the cereal to the apple mash. Serve.

3. Delicious Stewed Pear

Ingredients
1 pear
Honey, as per taste

Directions

- Wash and peel the pear and cut into pieces.
- Add the chopped pear in a pressure cooker, add a little water and let it whistle 2–3 times.
- Mash and add honey. Serve.

4. Nutritious Ragi

Ingredients

1 fig and 1 apricot, soaked overnight
2–3 almonds
2 tbsp. ragi powder
2 tsp. milk formula

Directions

- In a pan, add the ragi powder and water and cook on a slow flame.
- Once cooked it will achieve a thick consistency, add the fig and apricot, then add the formula and mix well.
- Mix in the almonds and serve.

5. Snacky Sooji (Wheat flour)

Ingredients

1 tbsp. dry flour

1 tbsp. ghee
1 tsp. elaichi powder
2 anjeer (figs), soaked overnight
2 tsp. milk formula
2 almonds
Salt, as per taste
1 tsp. sugar

Directions
- Roast dry flour till it turns yellow.
- Add a little ghee and fry the flour well.
- Add water. Add elaichi powder and anjeer. Stir till it starts to thicken.
- Add the formula milk and a pinch of salt and sugar. Mix well.
- Add the almonds and grind in a mixer. Serve.

6. Farm Fresh Oats Breakfast

Ingredients
2 tbsp. oats
1 tbsp. formula
2–3 almonds
A pinch of salt

Directions

- In a pan, put the oats, water and add a pinch of salt. Let it overcook.
- Add the almonds and formula.
- Blend well and serve.

SOUPS AND PUREES

1. The Baby Takhtani's Famous Bottle Gourd Soup

Ingredients

½ onion, roasted and chopped
¼ tsp. coriander powder
¼ tsp. cumin powder
¼ tsp. black pepper powder
1 small bowl of chopped bottle gourd
2 tbsp. moong dal
½ spoon of cream
½ cube of cheese
Salt, as per taste

Directions

- Roast the chopped onions in a cooker.
- Add the coriander, cumin and black pepper powder. Add the soaked moong dal and chopped bottle gourd in the cooker.
- Drop ½ a cube of cheese and add salt, as per taste, in the broth with ample water and let it whistle 3–4 times on a slow flame.
- Once cooked, add the cream.
- Blend it in the mixer and serve.

Note: At 4–5 months, the bottle gourd soup was the first thing my baby tried when shifting from milk to normal foods, but without cumin seeds, coriander powder, onions and black pepper. It was just the strained water of plain boiled bottle gourd. Once the baby got used to eating it, well into six months, the other ingredients were added. You can start off by feeding this soup to your baby once a month, then twice a day, between milk feeds.

2. Autumnal Pumpkin (Kaddu) Soup

Ingredients
¼ pumpkin
1 clove mashed garlic
1 small onion
1 small tomato
1 small potato
½ tsp. cumin seeds
½ tsp. turmeric powder
1 cup rice water
Salt and black-pepper powder, as per taste

Directions
- In a cooker add ghee and then put in the mashed garlic, cumin seeds and onion. Sauté well.

- Add the tomato and stir.
- Then add the turmeric and the black-pepper powder and mix it well.
- Add the chopped pumpkin and potato, rice water and salt to taste.
- After 2–3 whistles, let it cool.
- Blend in the mixer and serve.

3. Easy-Peasy Mix Vegetable Puree

Ingredients
10–12 pea pods
1 carrot
1 potato

Directions
- Peel the carrots and the potatoes and chop them into small cubes.
- Add peas to the mix and transfer the ingredients to a pressure cooker, with water. After about three whistles, turn off the gas.
- Blend the vegetables and the stock in a blender till it reaches the desired consistency.
- Cool and serve.

4. Winter Warming Sweet Potato and Pumpkin Soup

Ingredients
½ sweet potato
¼ pumpkin
½ onion
1 garlic clove
A pinch of ginger
A pinch of salt
A pinch of black pepper
1 tsp. fresh cream

Directions
- Wash and peel the sweet potato and pumpkin and chop them into small pieces.
- Add the ginger, garlic, onion, salt and pepper to a pan and boil together with all the chopped ingredients for 10 minutes.
- Allow it to cool and then blend it to a fine mixture.
- Add fresh cream to it and serve.

5. The All-Star Remedy Chicken Soup

Ingredients
100 gm boneless chicken
2 baby carrots

1 small potato
½ tomato
A pinch of salt
A pinch of black pepper

Directions
- Wash the chicken well and chop into small pieces.
- Add the chopped chicken, carrots, potato and halved tomato and let it boil for 5–8 minutes.
- Once it cools, add salt and black pepper, blend it well in the blender and serve.

6. Boosting Zucchini and Asparagus Soup

Ingredients
1 small zucchini
6 pieces of asparagus
1 garlic clove
A pinch of ginger
A pinch of salt
A pinch of black pepper
1 tbsp. fresh cream

Directions
- Wash and chop the zucchini and asparagus into small pieces.
- Boil the vegetables in a pan till the veggies are soft.

- Add salt, black pepper, ginger and garlic and blend in the blender.
- Add some fresh cream and the soup is ready to serve.

7. Grecian Broccoli and Olive Oil Puree

Ingredients
2 cups broccoli
1 white potato
1 tbsp. olive oil

Directions
- Wash and chop the broccoli into separate florets. Peel the potato and chop into small pieces.
- In a medium saucepan, bring water to a boil. Place the broccoli and potato in a steamer basket and place the basket into the boiling water. Let it steam for 10–12 minutes.
- Once cooled, add the steamed broccoli, potato and the olive oil in the blender and make a puree, by blending it until smooth. Add water from the steamer if needed.
- If additional seasoning is needed, feel free to add 1 tsp. chopped chives, 2–3 mint leaves, 1 tsp. cilantro or a squeeze of fresh lemon juice. Serve.

8. Creamy Green Soup

Ingredients
½ avocado
8–10 broccoli clusters
^{1}/3 onion
2 handfuls of spinach
1 tbsp. olive oil
1 tbsp. lemon juice
1 cup water
½ tsp. mint

Directions
- Wash and chop the broccoli.
- Add the broccoli and spinach to water and bring to a boil. When the spinach is slightly wilted and the broccoli turns light green, put them aside.
- Lightly fry the onions in olive oil.
- When the onion is cooked, add it along with the avocado, mint, lemon juice and boiled vegetables to a blender and blend.
- Add water depending on the desired consistency. Serve.

9. A Medley of Orange, Ginger and Sweet Potato Puree

Ingredients

1 sweet potato
1 drop of unsalted butter
1 tbsp. fresh orange juice
A dash of ginger

Directions

- Heat oven to 200°C. Wash and dry the potato and prick its skin with a fork in several places.
- Bake until potato is tender, approximately an hour.
- Peel the potato and discard the skin. Transfer potato to a bowl and mix until smooth. In a separate bowl, mix butter with orange juice and ginger.
- Bring both the mixes together, stir a few times and serve.

10. Well-seasoned Spinach Puree with Potatoes

Ingredients

30 ml milk
50 gm spinach
1 potato
10 gm butter

Directions

- Peel and cut the potato into cubes.
- Wash and coarsely chop the spinach.
- In a pan of boiling water, cook the potato and spinach for about 15 minutes.
- Drain and puree in a blender until the mixture is smooth.
- Beat in the butter and milk and serve.

11. Light Zucchini Puree

Ingredients
1 zucchini
4 tbsp. water
1 tbsp. olive oil

Directions

- Peel the zucchini, cut in half and remove the core and seeds.
- Put the prepared zucchini in a pan of boiling water and cover with a lid.
- When tender, mash with a fork, add the oil and the water.
- Cool and serve.

12. Healthy Clear Chicken Soup

Ingredients

300 gm chicken, with bones
¼ cup onion, chopped
¼ cup carrot, chopped
3–4 cloves garlic, smashed
2 bay leaves
2–3 sprigs thyme
4 cups of water
¼ tsp. black pepper, freshly cracked
Salt to taste
Spring onions, to garnish

Directions

- Wash the chicken and add it to a pressure cooker, along with the onion, garlic, carrot, bay leaves, thyme and water. Add salt and the freshly cracked black pepper and pressure cook on high heat, up to 1 whistle.
- Simmer for 10–12 minutes, on a low heat.
- Remove the pressure cooker from the heat. Let the pressure release and then pop open the cooker.
- Strain the soup using a soup strainer.
- Take out the chicken pieces and shred them into small pieces, discarding the bones. Add few

shredded pieces into each serving bowl and pour the clear soup from the top.

- Garnish with spring onions. Serve hot.

13. New York Special Avocado Puree

Ingredients
1 avocado
1 banana
1 tbsp. honey

Directions
- Peel the avocado and keep aside in a bowl.
- Peel the banana and mash together along with the avocado.
- Add honey and mix it well. Serve.

14. Playful Carrot Soup

Ingredients
2 tbsp. rice
½ carrot
¼ pepper
½ cheese cube
1 tsp. ghee
Salt, as per taste

Directions

- In a pressure cooker, add ghee, and then add the rice, carrot, pepper, cheese and salt. Add a little water.
- Let whistle 2–3 times.
- Once cool, blend it all in a mixer and serve.

LUNCH AND DINNER

1. Baby's Favourite Carrot and Potato Rice

Ingredients
2 tbsp. rice
½ carrot
½ potato
Salt

Directions
- Wash the rice and keep aside.
- Peel the carrot and remove the edges. Chop the carrot into fine pieces.
- Peel the potato and cut into small cubes.
- Add the potato and carrots to the rice. In a pressure cooker, add all the ingredients.
- Cook on a moderate flame and after 4 whistles, turn off the gas and allow it to cool.
- Mash the broth with a masher and add a generous pinch of salt. Serve.

2. One-Pot Wonder: Vegetable Khichdi

Ingredients
1 small potato

1 carrot
½ tomato
2 tbsp. moong dal
4 tbsp. rice

Directions
- Peel the potato and carrot and chop into cubes.
- Wash all the ingredients and place in a pressure cooker, with enough water to maintain a thick consistency.
- After 3 whistles, stir well and serve.

3. Shanta Aunty's Curd Curry (Dahi Curry)

Ingredients
1–2 garlic cloves
1 bowl curd
2 tsp. besan
5–6 curry leaves
½ tsp. coriander leaves
1 tbsp. ghee or oil
¼ tsp. cumin seeds
A pinch of asafoetida (hing)
A pinch of fenugreek seeds
A pinch of turmeric powder

Salt, as per taste

Jaggery, as per taste

Directions

- To the bowl of curd, add besan, turmeric, salt and water and mix well.
- Take a pan and add the oil, then add the asafoetida, cumin seeds, fenugreek seeds and curry leaves.
- Once it turns slightly brown, add the garlic.
- Add the beaten curd to it. Stir constantly so no lumps are formed.
- Garnish with coriander and serve.

4. Swadikha Thai Curry

Ingredients

1 cup assorted vegetables (cauliflower, baby corn, carrot)

1 tsp. ginger–garlic paste

½ onion

1 tbsp. oil

¼ cup coconut milk

1–2 cloves

A pinch of turmeric powder

A pinch of jeera powder

A pinch of coriander powder
Salt, as per taste
Black pepper, as per taste

Directions

- In a bowl, chop the veggies and soak in water for some time.
- In a pan, add oil and sauté chopped onion till golden brown.
- Add ginger–garlic paste and the soaked vegetables to the pan.
- Add the coconut milk, turmeric powder, jeera powder, coriander powder and salt and mix well.
- Once the vegetables are cooked, add the clove and black pepper and let it simmer for a while. Let it cool.
- Remove the clove and black pepper. Add to the blender and puree. Serve.

5. Egg Palak Powerhouse

Ingredients

2 tbsp. dal
2 tbsp. rice
1 potato, chopped

½ boiled egg
1 cup chopped spinach
A pinch of turmeric
A pinch of black pepper
1 tsp. ghee
Salt, as per taste

Directions
- In a cooker, add all the above ingredients, except the egg.
- Let it whistle 2–3 times. Mix well.
- Add the egg just before serving and mix well. Serve.

6. Mediterranean Veg. Pasta

Ingredients
1 cup boiled pasta, preferably overcooked
1 tsp. ghee or butter
½ white onion
1 cup of assorted greens (avocado, broccoli, asparagus, zucchini)
A pinch of salt
A pinch of black pepper
½ cheese cube
2 tsp. cream

Directions

- In a pan, add ghee and then add onions and let it cook. Sauté the vegetables. Add salt and pepper to it and let it cook properly.
- Add the boiled pasta in the pan and then add the cheese and white cream. Blend all the ingredients in a blender. Serve.

7. Delightfully Desi Paneer Paratha

Ingredients

1 cup flour
½ cup paneer (home-made)
A pinch of cumin (jeera) powder
A few coriander leaves
Pepper, as per taste
Salt, as per taste

Directions

- Mix the flour with some water and knead into a dough. Keep aside.
- In a bowl, crumble the paneer, add pepper, salt, coriander leaves and jeera powder. Mash well. This will be the filling.
- Take small rounds of dough and stuff the dough with the paneer filling.

- Roll the paratha and cook on a hot tawa. Apply ghee while turning over. Serve warm.

8. Protein-packed Chicken Curry Rice

Ingredients
1 chicken breast, boneless
⅓ onion
1 garlic clove
2 cinnamon sticks
1 clove
½ tomato
½ potato
1 bay leaf
A pinch of turmeric powder
A pinch of cumin powder (jeera)
A pinch of coriander powder
2 black pepper pods
Salt, as per taste
Coriander leaves

Directions
- Place the chicken in a cooker with a cup of water. Add bay leaf, onion, clove, cinnamon sticks, the garlic cloves, salt, black pepper pods, the piece of tomato and potato. Add the turmeric, cumin and

coriander powder. Cook in the cooker for 4–5 whistles.

- Let it overcook (don't let the water dry). Open the lid once cooked and remove the chicken and potato. Strain the cooked water along with the garlic. Remove all the whole spices.
- Put the strained water back into the cooker.
- Add the rice and let it cook for 2 whistles on a low flame.
- Once cooked, add the chicken and potato back in.
- Stir it well and let it soak in the spices.
- When ready to eat, place in a mixer and blend.
- Add little ghee in it. Garnish with the coriander leaves and serve.

9. Hearty Dal Tadka Khichdi

Ingredients
3 tbsp. yellow moong dal, soaked overnight
2 tbsp. rice
1 tbsp. ghee
½ onion
2 garlic cloves
3–4 curry leaves
½ potato
½ carrot

½ tomato
½ tsp. cumin seeds
½ tsp. coriander powder
½ tsp. turmeric powder
A pinch of asafoetida
A pinch of black pepper
Salt, as per taste

Directions

- In a cooker add ghee and then add asafoetida, onion, garlic clove and curry leaves. Once the ghee sputters, add dal and rice. Sauté well. Then add the cumin seeds, coriander powder, turmeric powder and black pepper.
- Mix well and then add the potato, carrot and tomato. Mix all. After 5–7 minutes, add little water and cook for 3–4 whistles on a low flame.
- Grind in a mixer and serve.

10. Vitamin-Rich Palak Paneer

Ingredients
2 tbsp. diced home-made paneer
1 garlic clove
A pinch of ginger
1 tbsp. ghee

½ onion

½ tomato

½ tsp. cumin seeds

¼ tsp. turmeric powder,

A pinch of black pepper powder

3–4 spinach leaves

Salt, as per taste

Directions

- Add ghee and cumin seeds to a cooker. Allow it to sputter. Add the onions, tomato, turmeric powder and black pepper powder. Sauté well.
- Add the spinach and paneer and let it cook for 2–3 whistles.
- Once cooked, blend in mixer and serve.

11. Traditional Marwari Khichdi

Ingredients

1 cup of 4–5 assorted and diced vegetables

⅓ cup rice.

1 tbsp. ghee

½ tsp. mustard and cumin seeds

2 garlic cloves

½ chopped onion

½ chopped tomato

A pinch of turmeric powder
A pinch of black pepper
Salt, as per taste

Directions

- Add ghee to a cooker. In the following order, add mustard and cumin seeds and the garlic; add the chopped onion and tomato; then add the turmeric and black pepper.
- Sauté well. Add the diced vegetables, rice, water and salt. Stir well. Let it cook for 3–4 whistles. Add more ghee and roasted garlic on top for flavour.
- Blend well in a mixer and serve.

12. Great Grandmama Amba's Curd Rice

Ingredients

1 cup rice
2 cups curd (or as per preference)
¼ cup milk
3–4 tsp. ghee
A pinch of asafoetida
A pinch of mustard seeds
3–4 curry leaves

Directions
- Cook the rice and keep aside. Add milk, curd and salt and mix well.
- In a small pan, heat the ghee, asafoetida, mustard seeds and curry leaves. Add this on top of the mixed curd rice and serve.

13. All-in-One Vegetable Khichdi

Ingredients
½ cup moong dal and rice, mixed and soaked
¼ potato, chopped
¼ carrot, chopped
¼ tomato, chopped
A pinch of turmeric powder
Salt, as per taste

Directions
- Add the soaked moong dal and rice to a cooker.
- Add the vegetables, turmeric powder and salt. Let it whistle 2 or 3 times. Your hearty vegetable khichdi is ready to be served.

DESSERTS

1. Creamy Crunchy Fruit Yoghurt with Biscuits

Ingredients
4 tbsp. plain yoghurt
¼ banana
1 segment of an orange
2 tsp. crumbled biscuits

Directions
- Peel the orange. Mash all the fruits together with a fork.
- Add the yoghurt and biscuits and mix well. Serve

2. Lip-smacking Apricot

Ingredients
1 can apricots in fruit juice
50 gm soft cheese
50 gm yoghurt

Directions
- Smash the apricots to your desired consistency. Bring together the cheese and yoghurt and mix them.

- Add 3 tbsp. of the apricot pulp to cheese and yoghurt mixture. Mix well and serve.

3. Valina's Famous Bread Pudding

Ingredients
6 slices of bread
2 eggs
1.5 cup of milk
3 tbsp. sugar, more for caramel
1 tsp. vanilla essence
1 tsp. black cardamom powder

Directions
- Take 6 slices of bread and cut the side corners. Blend into a mixture until it's soft and keep aside in a bowl.
- Then, take 2 eggs and beat them. Add the milk, sugar, fresh black cardamom powder and a little vanilla essence into the beaten eggs. Mix till there are no lumps.
- Add the bread mixture to the egg mixture and fold it together. Set aside for 10–15 minutes to soak.
- Place a little sugar in a pan to make caramel. Once the caramelized sugar is ready, pour it into the dish. It should harden slightly. Then pour the bread pudding batter which was kept aside.

- Follow the double boiler method by placing the bread pudding bowl in a larger container with water. Cover it with aluminium foil.
- Bring the water to a boil.
- After 30 minutes, remove the foil and check whether it's cooked through. If the consistency is not the same in all areas keep it for 40 minutes on a low flame, finishing with 5 minutes on a high flame, alternating as necessary. Serve.

4. Refreshing Mango Sooji

Ingredients

¼ cup sooji
1 mango sliced
3–4 apricots, soaked overnight
2–3 anjeer
1 tsp. ghee
2 tsp. formula powder
2–3 almonds, soaked overnight

Directions

- In a bowl add the roasted sooji, sliced mango pieces, anjeer, apricots, formula powder, ghee, almonds and water. Put all the ingredients in a blender and blend well. Serve.

5. Baby's Sweet-tooth: Gajar ka Halwa

Ingredients
1 grated carrot
1 tsp. ghee
1 tsp. elaichi powder
1 tsp. sugar
1 tbsp. paneer
2 tsp. milk formula
Salt, as per taste

Directions
- In a kadai, add ghee, carrot, elaichi powder, water, sugar and salt. Let it boil well.
- Add the paneer and mix well, till semi-dry.
- Add the milk formula and cook it a little longer.
- Once cooled, blend it in a mixer and serve.

6. May Mango Mania Souffle

Ingredients
1 small cup of mango cubes
2 tbsp. curd

Directions
- Add the mango cubes and curd to the blender and blend well. Serve.

7. Alleppey's Semolina Appam

Ingredients
1 finely chopped onion
1 tsp. chopped coriander
3–4 curry leaves
2 tbsp. yoghurt
½ cup semolina flour

Directions
- Finely chop the onions, coriander and curry leaves.
- Mix some yoghurt and semolina flour together (the consistency should be thick).
- Leave aside for 10 minutes.
- Put some ghee in a pan, spread the yoghurt-semolina mixture and cook for 5–7 minutes.
- Let it cool and serve.

8. Jelly

Ingredients
1 packet jelly powder
1 small bowl of freshly cut fruits
2 glasses of water

Directions

- Take half a glass of water and mix in the jelly powder.
- Heat one glass of water in a pan.
- Once the water is boiled, add the jelly powder, mix thoroughly and remove from heat.
- Transfer the jelly into a bowl and let it cool.
- Add freshly cut fruits and refrigerate.
- Serve cold.

9. Doodhi Payasam

Ingredients

2 bottle gourds (doodhi)
2 tsp. ghee
½ cup fresh coconut water
½ tsp flaxseed (alsi) powder
Sugar or jaggery

Directions

- Take two tender bottle-gourds (doodhis), wash them thoroughly, scrape into very thin slices and put in a pan.
- Add the ghee and a bit of water and let the gourds cook.

- Once the water has dried, add fresh coconut water, stirring thoroughly.
- Add a little alsi powder and some sugar or jaggery (as per choice).
- Stir till the sugar/jaggery has melted.
- Remove from the heat and let it cool before serving.

10. Caramel Custard

Ingredients
2 cups of milk
1 egg
3 tsp. sugar
1 packet caramel powder
1 tbsp. water

Directions
- Take a bowl, put in half a cup of milk, the egg and the caramel powder.
- Mix thoroughly with a hand blender.
- Take a pan and pour in the rest of the milk. Keep the pan on the gas and let it boil.
- Once the milk has boiled, add the batter into the pan, stirring thoroughly.
- Remove from heat once it reaches a thick consistency. Make sure no lumps have formed.

- Take a pan, add the sugar and 1 spoonful water. Stir till the sugar is golden brown.
- Take a bowl, spread the caramelized sugar into the bowl and fold the batter into it. Keep aside until the batter is cool and refrigerate before serving.

11. Pancake

Ingredients

½ cup of wheat flour
1 egg
½ cup milk
A pinch of salt
Butter/maple syrup/jam, to taste

Directions

- Take a bowl, put in the wheat flour and the egg.
- Stir it properly with a spoon.
- Add some milk to the mixture till the batter reaches a thick consistency.
- Add a pinch of salt.
- Take a pan, add the batter and let it cook on a slow flame.
- Remove once cooked.
- Add butter/maple syrup/jam on top (as per choice).

For Babies 1 Year Onwards

BREAKFAST AND SNACKS

1. Best Friend's Special French Toast

Ingredients
3–4 tbsp. milk
¼ spoon of sugar
1 cup of wheat flour
2 slices of bread
½ spoon of butter or oil
A pinch of black pepper

Directions
- Place the milk, sugar, wheat flour and black pepper in a small bowl and mix it well.

- Cut the slices of bread into 2 pieces each and dip into the mixture.
- Add butter to a non-stick pan and fry the dipped bread on a slow flame. Serve once it turns slightly golden brown.

2. Light and Fruity Apple Porridge

Ingredients
2–3 tsp. oats
½ grated apple
½ tbsp. sugar
A pinch of black-sugar powder

Directions
- In a pressure cooker wash the oats, and let whistle 3–4 times.
- Add the grated apple and sugar to the oats. Cook on low flame for a while and your apple oats porridge is ready to be served.

3. Potassium Packed Banana Porridge

Ingredients
2–3 tsp. oats
1 banana
½ tbsp. sugar

Directions

- In a pressure cooker wash the oats, and let it whistle 3–4 times.
- Add the banana and sugar to the oats. Cook on low flame for a while and your banana oats porridge is ready to be served.

4. Wonderful Pear Porridge

Ingredients

2–3 tsp. oats
½ pear
½ tbsp. sugar

Directions

- In a pressure cooker wash the oats, and let it whistle 3–4 times.
- Add the pear and sugar to the oats.
- Cook on low flame for a while and your pear oats porridge is ready to be served.

5. Calcium Packed Milk Porridge

Ingredients

2–3 tsp. oats
½ cup of milk
½ tbsp. sugar
A pinch of cardamom powder (elaichi)

Directions

- In a pressure cooker wash the oats, and let it whistle 3–4 times.
- Add the milk, cardamom powder and sugar to the oats.
- Cook on low flame for 2–4 minutes and your milk porridge is ready to be served.

6. Rukmini Mami's Semolina Upma (Sooji Ka Upma)

Ingredients

½ cup semolina
½ tbsp. ghee or oil
¼ tsp. mustard seeds
3–4 curry leaves
½ tsp. urad dal
1 tbsp. chopped coriander
1 onion, chopped
Salt, as per taste

Directions

- Sauté the semolina/sooji in a pan properly, but do not let it brown.
- In another pan, add oil or ghee, add the mustard seeds, curry leaves and urad dal. Once it crackles, add the chopped onions. Cook until pink.

- Add the water and the salt. Let it boil for 5 minutes.
- After mixing it well, add the sautéed semolina to the pan and mix well. Sprinkle the finely chopped coriander on top and serve.

7. Fun Vegetable Semolina Upma

Ingredients
½ cup semolina
½ carrot, finely chopped
2–3 beans
A handful of peas
½ onion, chopped
½ tomato, chopped
1 tbsp. oil or ghee
¼ tsp. mustard seeds
3–4 curry leaves
½ tsp. urad dal

Directions
- Sauté the semolina for a few minutes and keep aside.
- In another pan add oil and mustard seeds, curry leaves and urad dal. Sauté it and then add the onion and tomato to it and let it cook for 5 minutes.
- Add the vegetables and cook again for some time.

- Add ½ cup water and let it boil.
- Add the sautéed semolina to the cooked vegetables. Cook on low flame for some time.
- Mix well and serve.

8. Continental Potato Wrap

Ingredients
1 tbsp. cumin seeds
½ tbsp. mustard seeds
1 small onion, chopped
1 tbsp. ginger–garlic paste
1 potato
½ tbsp. turmeric powder
½ tbsp. amchur powder
¼ tbsp. garam masala powder
½ cup of water
½ cup of flour, to which you may add ¼ tsp. salt
1 tbsp. oil

Directions
- In a pan add oil and sauté cumin seeds, mustard seeds, chopped onion and ginger–garlic paste. Fry well. Add the spices and mix well.
- Add enough water and salt to the flour so it achieves the consistency of dosa batter.

- Mix the potato in with the rest of the mixture till cooked.
- In a non-stick pan, pour refined oil and spread the flour batter like you would to make a dosa. Fill the stuffing in the centre. Fold it properly and fry on a low flame. Your tasty breakfast is ready to be served.

9. Sweet Semolina Halwa

Ingredients
½ cup semolina
3–4 tbsp. ghee
¼ cup of milk
2 tbsp. sugar
A pinch of cardamom

Directions
- In a pan add the ghee and sauté the semolina till it turns golden brown.
- Add the milk, sugar and cardamom. Cook for 3–4 minutes. The sooji halwa is ready to serve

10. Madurai Special Semolina Idli

Ingredients
½ cup semolina
2–3 tbsp. curd
½ tsp. oil
Salt, as per taste

Directions
- Mix semolina, curd and salt and keep it aside for 15 minutes.
- Brush the idli mould in the idli stand with oil and pour the batter into them. Let it cook for 10–15 minutes. Serve.

11. Tangy Semolina Dosa

Ingredients
½ cup semolina
2–3 tbsp. curd
Salt to taste
Assorted vegetables (optional)

Directions
- Spread oil in a pan on a low flame. Mix all the ingredients. Spread the mixture on the pan and cook it in low flame. Serve.

12. Super Duper Oats

Plain oats

Ingredients
2 tbsp. oats
½ cup water
½ cup milk
½ tbsp. sugar

Directions
- In a pan sauté the oats for some time.
- Add the water, milk and sugar to the oats and cook for 10–12 minutes. Serve.

Banana oats

Ingredients
2–3 tbsp. oats
½ cup water
½ cup milk
½ tbsp. sugar
½ banana

Directions
- Sauté the oats in a pan for some time.

- Add the water, milk, sugar and mashed banana to the oats and cook for 10–12 minutes. Serve.

Apple oats

Ingredients

2–3 tbsp. oats
½ cup water
½ cup milk
½ tbsp. sugar
½ apple, grated

Directions

- Sauté the oats in a pan for some time.
- Add the water, milk, sugar and grated apple to the oats and cook for 5 minutes. Serve.

Pear oats

Ingredients

2–3 tbsp. oats
½ cup water
½ cup milk
½ tbsp. sugar
½ pear

Directions

- Sauté the oats in a pan for some time.
- Add the water, milk, sugar and grated pear to the oats and cook for 5 minutes. Serve.

Milk oats

Ingredients

2–3 tbsp. oats
½ cup water
½ cup milk
½ tbsp. sugar

Directions

- Sauté the oats in a pan for some time.
- Add the water and cook for 2–3 minutes. Add milk and sugar and cook for 5 minutes. Milk Oats is ready to be served.

13. Marwari Oats Chilla

Ingredients

2–3 tbsp. oats
½ onion, chopped
½ carrot, grated
2 beans, finely chopped

175

½ tomato, chopped
½ capsicum, chopped
Salt, as per taste

Directions
- Cook all the vegetables and the oats on a medium flame for 5 minutes.
- Once cooled, blend in a mixer to a medium consistency. Then brush some oil or ghee on to a pan and spread the batter like you would with a dosa. Cook on low flame and serve when ready.

14. Surprising Mix Vegetable Idli

Ingredients
½ carrot, grated
2–3 beans, finely chopped
1 cup idli batter
1 tsp. salt

Directions
- Mix all the chopped vegetables with the idli batter. Add a pinch of salt.
- Brush the idli stand with oil and pour the mixed batter in. Let it cook for 10–15 minutes. Serve.

15. School Tiffin Cheese Sandwich

Ingredients
2 slices of bread
1 slice cheese
1 tsp. butter

Directions
- Take 2 slices of bread and apply butter on one side of each. Place the cheese slice in between the bread. Serve.

16. Mamma's Favourite Summer Cucumber Sandwich

Ingredients
2 slices of bread
1 small cucumber, thinly sliced
1 tsp. butter
Salt, as per taste
Pepper, as per taste

Directions
- Take the bread and cut into round shapes with a mould or a knife. Apply butter on one side of each of the slices.

- Place the thinly sliced cucumber on the buttered bread. Sprinkle a pinch of salt and pepper over it and serve.

17. Filling Potato Sandwich

Ingredients
2 slices of bread
1 small potato, boiled and thinly sliced
1 tsp. butter
Salt, as per taste
Pepper, as per taste

Directions
- Take the slices of bread and cut them into round shapes with a mould or a knife. Apply butter on one side of the slice.
- Place the thinly sliced potato on the buttered bread. Sprinkle a pinch of salt and pepper over it and serve.

LUNCH AND DINNER

1. Popeye's Power Spinach Khichdi

Ingredients
1 bunch spinach
1 tbsp. ghee or oil
2–3 garlic cloves, mashed
3 tbsp. rice
A pinch of cumin seeds
A pinch of asafoetida

Directions
- Chop palak finely. Pour the ghee or oil in the pressure cooker. Add the cumin seeds, asafoetida and mashed garlic. Once the oil starts to sputter, add the palak and rice and sauté for 2–3 minutes.
- Add a cup of water and let it cook. After 3–4 whistles, turn the gas off. Cool slightly and serve.

2. Thanksgiving Special Pumpkin Khichdi

Ingredients
50 gm pumpkin
50 gm rice
1 tbsp. oil or ghee

2–3 garlic cloves, mashed
Salt, as per taste
A pinch of asafoetida

Directions
- In a pressure cooker add oil, a pinch of asafoetida, mashed garlic and sauté.
- Add the rice and pumpkin and stir well.
- Add 1 cup of water and close the lid. Take it off the heat after 3–4 whistles. Let it cool and then serve.

3. Simple and Easy Carrot Potato Khichdi

Ingredients
1 small carrot
1 small potato
1 tbsp. ghee or oil
2–3 garlic cloves, mashed
3 tbsp. rice
A pinch of cumin seeds
A pinch of asafoetida

Directions
- Chop the carrot and potato into small pieces.
- In a pressure cooker, add the spoon of oil or ghee, a pinch of asafoetida, cumin seeds and mashed

garlic. Immediately, add the carrot, potato, rice, salt and mix well for 2–3 minutes. Add 1 cup of water and let it whistle 3–4 times. Serve.

4. Veggie Delight Mixed Vegetables Khichdi

Ingredients
1 small carrot
1 small potato
2–3 beans
2 cauliflower florets
1 tbsp. ghee or oil
2–3 garlic cloves, mashed
3 tbsp. rice
A pinch of cumin seeds
A pinch of asafoetida
Salt, as per taste

Directions
- Chop carrot, potato, beans and cauliflower into small pieces.
- In the pressure cooker, add the spoon of oil or ghee, a pinch of asafoetida, cumin seeds and mashed garlic. Immediately, add the carrot, potato, beans, cauliflower, rice and salt and mix well for 2–3 minutes.
- Add 1 cup of water and let it whistle 3–4 times. Serve.

5. Protein Punch Yellow Split Lentils Khichdi

Ingredients
3–4 tbsp. rice
3–4 tbsp. yellow split lentils
1 tbsp. ghee or oil
1–2 garlic cloves, mashed
A pinch of asafoetida
¼ tsp. cumin seed
Salt, as per taste

Directions
- In a pressure cooker, add the spoon of oil or ghee, a pinch of asafoetida, cumin seeds and mashed garlic.
- Add the lentils, rice, salt and mix well for 2–3 minutes. Add a cup of water and let it whistle 2–3 times. Serve.

6. Strengthening Whole Green Dal Khichdi

Ingredients
2–3 tbsp. rice
2–3 tbsp. green split lentils
1 spoon of ghee or oil
¼ tsp. cumin seed

1–2 garlic cloves, mashed

A pinch of asafoetida

Salt, as per taste

Directions

- In a pressure cooker add the spoon of oil or ghee, a pinch of asafoetida, cumin seeds and mashed garlic.
- Add the lentils, rice and salt and mix well for 2–3 minutes. Add a cup of water and let it whistle 2–3 times. Serve.

7. Sweet Potato Khichdi

Ingredients

1 sweet potato

2–3 tbsp. rice

1 tbsp. ghee or oil

A pinch of asafoetida

¼ tsp. cumin seeds

1–2 garlic cloves, mashed

Salt, as per taste

Directions

- Chop the sweet potato into small pieces.
- In a pressure cooker, add the spoon of oil or ghee, a pinch of asafoetida, cumin seeds and mashed

garlic. Add the sweet potato, rice and salt and mix well for 2–3 minutes.

- Add 1 cup of water and let whistle 2–3 times. Serve.

8. Punjabi Special Paneer Peas (Paneer Mutter)

Ingredients
50 gm paneer
50 gm peas
½ onion
½ tomato
3–4 garlic cloves
A pinch of ginger
1 tbsp. oil
½ tsp. cumin seeds
½ tsp. turmeric powder
½ tsp. garam masala
A pinch of asafoetida

Directions
- Cut the paneer into small pieces. Make a paste of the onion, tomato, garlic and ginger.
- Heat oil in a pan. Add the cumin seeds, asafoetida, turmeric powder, garam masala and fry well. Add the paste and fry.

- Finally, add the peas and paneer. Sauté all the ingredients nicely. Add a cup of water and let it simmer for 5–7 minutes. Once the peas are cooked, your paneer mutter is ready to be served

9. Dilliwala Butter Paneer

Ingredients
50 gm paneer, cubed
1 tomato
1 tbsp. ginger–garlic paste
1 tbsp. butter
1 bay leaf
1 cardamom
1 cinnamon stick
1 onion, finely chopped
½ tsp. turmeric powder
½ tsp. cumin powder
½ tsp. garam masala powder
½ tsp. coriander powder
Salt, as per taste

Directions
- In a pan add butter and then add the bay leaf, cardamom and cinnamon stick.
- Add the chopped onion and fry till golden brown.

- Add the ginger–garlic paste and the tomato and fry nicely for 3–4 minutes.
- Add the turmeric, cumin, coriander and garam masala powders. Add salt to taste. Mix well.
- Finally, add the cubed paneer. Add water and let it cook on a slow flame for 5–7 minutes. Garnish with chopped coriander and serve.

10. Daddy's Favourite Rajma

Ingredients
½ cup red kidney beans (rajma), soaked for 3–4 hrs
½ onion, ground into a paste
½ tomato, ground into a paste
1 tsp. ginger–garlic paste
A pinch of asafoetida
1 tsp. oil
½ tsp. cumin seeds
2–3 bay leaves
½ tsp. cumin powder
½ tsp. garam masala powder
½ tsp. coriander powder
Chopped coriander leaves, to garnish
Salt, as per taste

Directions

- Boil the soaked rajma till they are cooked.
- Heat the oil in a pan. Add cumin seeds, bay leaves and sauté. Then add the onion and tomato paste, ginger–garlic paste and all the spices and fry them well. Add salt to taste.
- Once they appear to be cooked, add the rajma to the pan and mix well. Add water and let it cook on a slow flame for 2 whistles.
- Garnish with chopped coriander leaves and serve.

11. Flavourful Black Eye Beans

Ingredients

½ cup of black-eyed beans, soaked for 3–4 hrs
½ onion, ground into a paste
½ tomato, ground into a paste
1 tsp. ginger–garlic paste
A pinch of asafoetida
1 tsp. oil
½ tsp. cumin seeds
2–3 bay leaves
½ tsp. cumin powder
½ tsp. garam masala powder
½ tsp. coriander powder

Chopped coriander leaves, to garnish
Salt, as per taste

Directions

- Boil the soaked black-eyed beans till they appear to be cooked.
- Heat oil in a pan, add cumin seeds, bay leaves and sauté.
- Add the onion and tomato paste, ginger–garlic paste and all the spices and fry well. Add salt as per taste. Once nicely cooked, add the black-eyed beans to the pan and mix well.
- Add water and let it cook on a slow flame for 2 whistles.
- Garnish with chopped coriander leaves and serve.

12. Chatpata Chickpeas (Chhole)

Ingredients

½ cup of chickpeas (chhole), soaked for 3–4 hrs
½ onion, ground into a paste
½ tomato, ground into a paste
1 tsp. ginger–garlic paste
A pinch of asafoetida
1 tsp. oil
½ tsp. cumin seeds

2–3 bay leaves
½ tsp. cumin powder
½ tsp. garam masala powder
½ tsp. coriander powder
Chopped coriander leaves, to garnish
Salt, as per taste

Directions

- Boil the soaked chickpeas till cooked.
- Heat oil in a pan. Add cumin seeds, bay leaves and sauté.
- Add the onion and tomato paste, ginger–garlic paste and all the spices and fry well. Add salt as per taste.
- Once nicely cooked, add the chickpeas to the pan and mix well.
- Add water and let it cook on a slow flame for 2 whistles.
- Garnish with chopped coriander leaves and serve.

13. Hearty Red Lentils

Ingredients

½ cup red lentils
½ onion, finely chopped
1 tomato, made into a paste

2–3 cloves of garlic, made into a paste
1 tbsp. oil
½ tsp. cumin seeds
½ tsp. cumin powder
½ tsp. garam masala powder
½ tsp. coriander powder
Salt, as per taste

Directions

- Heat oil in the pressure cooker and add the cumin seeds, onion, tomato paste and garlic paste and sauté well.
- Add the cumin powder, coriander powder, garam masala powder and salt and fry well.
- Add the red lentils and mix well.
- Add a cup of water and let it cook for 3–4 whistles on a moderate flame. Serve.

14. Vegetable Chapatti with a Pumpkin Twist

Ingredients
50 gm pumpkin, chopped
1 tsp. oil
A pinch of asafoetida
2–3 grains of fenugreek
2–3 garlic cloves, mashed

½ tsp. turmeric powder
½ tsp. cumin powder
½ tsp. coriander powder
Salt, as per taste

Directions

- Heat oil in a pressure cooker. Add asafoetida, fenugreek seeds, mashed garlic, turmeric powder, cumin powder, coriander powder and salt. Sauté nicely.
- Add the chopped pumpkin and fry well.
- Add ½ cup water and cook for 2–3 whistles. Serve with chapatti or rice.

15. Everyday Basics: Potato Gravy

Ingredients
1 potato, chopped
1 onion, finely chopped
½ tomato, mashed
½ tbsp. ginger–garlic paste
1 tsp. oil or ghee
½ tsp. cumin seeds
A pinch of asafoetida
½ tsp. turmeric powder
½ tsp. coriander powder

½ tsp. cumin powder
¼ tsp. garam masala
Salt, as per taste

Directions

- Fry the finely chopped onions, asafoetida and cumin seeds well in a pressure cooker.
- Add the ginger–garlic paste and mashed tomato and fry for 2–3 minutes.
- Add the turmeric powder, coriander powder, cumin powder, garam masala and salt. Sauté well. Let it whistle 2–3 times after adding a little water. Serve.

16. Comforting Cottage Cheese Gravy

Ingredients

1 cup paneer, chopped into small squares
½ onion, finely chopped
½ tomato, mashed
½ tsp. ginger–garlic paste
1 tsp. oil
A pinch of asafoetida
½ tsp. turmeric powder
½ tsp. coriander powder
½ tsp. cumin powder

¼ tsp. garam masala

Salt, as per taste

Directions

- Heat oil in a pan and fry the chopped onions, ginger–garlic paste and tomato. Sauté well.
- Add the asafoetida, coriander powder, turmeric powder, cumin powder and garam masala. Fry for 5 minutes.
- Add 1 cup of water and let it come to a boil.
- Add the cubed paneer and let it cook on a slow flame for 3–4 minutes. Serve.

17. Little Nizam's Paneer Kofta

Ingredients

For Kofta

1 cup paneer, mashed

1 potato, boiled and mashed

1 tsp. ginger–garlic paste

Salt, as per taste

Directions

- Mix all the ingredients well.
- Make into small round balls and fry. Keep aside.

For Gravy

½ onion

1 tbsp. oil

1 tsp. ginger–garlic paste

1 tomato, mashed

5–6 cashew nuts

½ tsp. turmeric powder

½ tsp. coriander powder

½ tsp. cumin powder

¼ tsp. garam masala

Salt, as per taste

Chopped coriander, for garnish

Directions

- In a pan, add oil, onion, mashed tomato, ginger–garlic paste, cashews, and all the spices and sauté well.
- Once cooked, add salt and water and let it come to a boil.
- Add the fried kofta balls to the gravy and let it cook on slow flame for 2–3 minutes.
- Garnish with chopped coriander and serve.

18. Crumbly Paneer Bhurji

Ingredients

1 cup paneer, grated

1 onion, finely chopped
1 tomato, finely chopped
½ tsp. turmeric powder
¼ tsp. garam masala
½ tsp. cumin seeds
1 tbsp. oil

Directions
- Heat oil in a pan, sauté the cumin seeds and chopped onion for 1–2 minutes.
- Add the turmeric powder, garam masala and tomato.
- Once cooked, add the grated paneer and salt to taste.
- Mix well and let it simmer for some time. Serve.

19. Mouth-watering Chicken Curry

Ingredients
1 cup boneless chicken
½ onion
½ tomato
½ tsp. ginger–garlic paste
1 tbsp. oil
½ tsp. cumin seeds
1 bay leaf

1 clove
1 cinnamon stick
½ tsp. coriander powder
½ tsp. cumin powder
½ tsp. turmeric
¼ tsp. garam masala
Salt, as per taste

Directions

- Sauté the bay leaf, cinnamon stick, clove, cumin seeds, onion, tomato and ginger–garlic paste well in a cooker.
- Add the chicken, salt, coriander powder, turmeric powder and garam masala powder and fry well for 3–4 minutes. Add 1 cup of water and let it whistle 3–4 times. Serve.

20. Zesty Dry Chicken

Ingredients
1–2 pieces of chicken
1 onion, chopped
1 tomato, chopped
½ tbsp. ginger–garlic paste
1–2 tbsp. oil
½ tsp. cumin seeds

½ tsp. khada masala
½ tsp. coriander powder
½ tsp. cumin powder
½ tsp. turmeric
¼ tsp. garam masala
Salt, as per taste

Directions

- Heat oil in a pan. Fry the onions till they turn brown. Add the tomato, ginger–garlic paste, cumin powder, khada masala, turmeric powder, coriander powder, garam masala and salt. Cook well.
- Add the chicken. Fry nicely and cook on a slow flame for 15 minutes till chicken is tender and cooked through. Your dry chicken is ready to be served.

21. Little Deol's Favourite (Secret) Egg Curry

Ingredients
1–2 boiled eggs
1 onion
1 small tomato
½ tsp. ginger–garlic paste
1 tbsp. oil
½ tsp. cumin seeds
A pinch of asafoetida

½ tsp. coriander powder
½ tsp. cumin powder
½ tsp. turmeric
Salt, as per taste

Directions
- In a pan, add oil and sauté onion, tomato and ginger–garlic paste.
- Add asafoetida, coriander powder, cumin powder, turmeric powder and salt. Stir well.
- Add 1 cup of water. Once it comes to a boil, add the boiled eggs to the gravy. Serve.

22. Baby's Power Lunch: Chicken in Curd

Ingredients
1–2 chicken pieces
1–2 tsp. curd
½ tsp. ginger–garlic paste
½ tsp. coriander powder
½ tsp. cumin powder
½ tsp. turmeric powder
¼ tsp. garam masala
Chopped coriander leaves, to garnish
1 tbsp. ghee or oil
Salt, as per taste

Directions

- Marinate the chicken with curd and all the ingredients above. Keep aside for an hour.
- In a cooker add ghee or oil. Then add the marinated chicken. Fry well for 4–5 minutes. Add a little water and let whistle 3–4 times. Serve.

23. Quick and Easy Minced Chicken

Ingredients

½ cup minced chicken
½ onion, finely chopped
1 tomato, finely chopped
½ tsp. ginger–garlic paste
1 tsp. oil
½ tsp. cumin seeds
1 bay leaf
1 clove
1 cinnamon stick
½ tsp. cumin powder
½ tsp. coriander powder
½ tsp. turmeric powder
¼ tsp. garam masala
Salt, as per taste

Directions

- Heat oil in a cooker and add the clove, bay leaf and cinnamon stick. Add the onions to the spices and fry well.
- Add the minced chicken and mix together.
- Add the tomato, ginger–garlic paste, cumin powder, coriander powder, turmeric powder, garam masala and salt. Fry well for 2–3 minutes. Cook for 2–3 whistles. Your minced chicken is ready to be served.

24. Refreshing Matki (Sprouts)

Ingredients

½ cup matki sprouts, soaked for an hour
½ onion, finely chopped
½ tomato, finely chopped
½ tsp. ginger–garlic paste
1 tsp. oil
½ tsp. cumin seeds
½ tsp. cumin powder
¼ tsp. garam masala
½ tsp. coriander powder
Salt, as per taste

Directions
- Fry the chopped onions, tomato, cumin seeds, ginger–garlic paste in a cooker for 3–4 minutes.
- Add the cumin powder, garam masala, coriander powder, matki and salt. Sauté and let it whistle 3–4 times. Mix and serve.

25. Wholesome Black Lentils (Urad Dal)

Ingredients
½ cup black lentils (urad dal), soaked for 2–3 hrs
½ onion, finely chopped
½ tomato, finely chopped
½ tsp. ginger–garlic paste
1 tbsp. oil
½ tsp. cumin seeds
½ tsp. cumin powder
¼ tsp. garam masala
½ tsp. coriander powder
Salt, as per taste

Directions
- Heat oil in a cooker. Add the cumin seeds, onion, tomato, ginger–garlic paste and fry well.
- Add all the spices and sauté.

- Finally, add the black lentils and mix well. Add salt to taste. Add water and let it whistle 2–3 times. Serve.

26. Hong Kong Special Vegetable Fried Rice

Ingredients
2 tbsp. rice, boiled
½ carrot, chopped
½ capsicum, chopped
1–2 beans, chopped
1–2 spring onions
A pinch of black pepper
1 tbsp. refined oil
Salt, as per taste

Directions
- Add oil to a small wok. Fry the vegetables well and add salt and black pepper.
- After the vegetables are half cooked, add the rice and mix well.
- Sprinkle on the chopped spring onion as garnish. Serve.

27. The House Speciality: Rasam

Ingredients

½ tomato, chopped
1–2 garlic cloves
A pinch of ginger
1–2 black pepper pods
A pinch of asafoetida
A pinch of cumin seeds
A pinch of turmeric powder
A pinch of rasam masala powder
1 tbsp. refined oil
Curry leaves
Coriander
Salt, as per taste

Directions

- Heat oil in a pan and fry the chopped tomato. Add the garlic, curry leaves, black pepper and ginger. Mix well.
- Add the spices and a cup of water with the salt. Let it cook for 6–7 minutes.
- Garnish with chopped coriander and serve.

28. Cooling Ridge Vegetable (Turai)

Ingredients
½ onion
½ tomato, finely chopped
½ cup ridge gourd, chopped
1–2 garlic cloves, mashed
A pinch of asafoetida
A pinch of cumin seeds
A pinch of turmeric powder
A pinch of coriander powder
1 tbsp. refined oil
Salt, as per taste

Directions
- Add oil in a pan and sauté the asafoetida, cumin seeds, onion, tomato and garlic.
- Add the chopped vegetables and the spices. Mix together.
- Add water and let it cook on slow flame for 4–5 minutes. The cooling turai is ready to serve.

29. Summer Special Snake Gourd

Ingredients
1 tbsp. moong dal

20 gm snake gourd, chopped
1 tbsp. refined oil
A pinch of asafoetida
A pinch of cumin seeds
A pinch of turmeric powder
1–2 garlic cloves
Salt, as per taste

Directions
- In a cooker add oil, asafoetida and cumin seeds.
- Add all the above ingredients and fry well for 2–3 minutes.
- Add a cup of water and cook on a medium flame for 2–3 whistles. Serve.

30. Houseful Mixed Vegetables

Ingredients
½ carrot
½ capsicum
½ potato
1–2 beans
1–2 florets of cauliflower, chopped into small pieces
1 tsp. ghee or oil
A pinch of asafoetida
A pinch of cumin seeds

A pinch of turmeric powder

A pinch of coriander powder

A pinch of garam masala powder

Salt, as per taste

Directions

- Heat 1 tsp. ghee/oil in the pressure cooker. Add the asafoetida and cumin seeds. Let it splutter.
- Add the mixed vegetables and the spices.
- Add water. Cook for 2–3 whistles or for 10 minutes in a pan.

31. Bengal Style Moong Dal

Ingredients

1 tsp. oil or ghee

2–3 tbsp. moong dal

1–2 garlic cloves, mashed

A pinch of asafoetida

1 tsp. cumin seeds

¼ tsp. turmeric

Salt, as per taste

Directions

- In a pressure cooker add 1 spoon of oil or ghee, a pinch of asafoetida, cumin seeds, mashed garlic.

Add the moong dal, salt, turmeric and mix well for 2–3 minutes.

- Add 1 cup of water and let it whistle 2–3 times. Ready to serve.

32. Dreamgirl's Sweet Pongal

Ingredients
½ cup rice
¼ cup moong dal
½ cup jaggery
4–5 cashew nuts
10–12 raisins

Directions
- In a pressure cooker add ghee, rice, dal and jaggery and stir well.
- Add the cashew and raisins and fry well. Add 2 cups of water and cook for 3–4 whistles. Serve.

33. South Indian Pongal

Ingredients
3 tbsp. rice
2 tbsp. moong dal
2 tsp. ghee

A pinch of asafoetida
4–5 curry leaves
Garlic cloves, mashed
4–5 pods of black pepper
4–5 cashew nuts
4–5 raisins

Directions

- In a pressure cooker add ghee, asafoetida, curry leaves, mashed garlic, pepper.
- When slightly brown, add rice and dal. Stir well.
- Add cashew and raisin and fry it. Add 1 cup of water and salt to taste. Cook for 3–4 whistles and serve.

34. Chennai Special Sambar

Ingredients

1 tbsp. toor dal
1 small bowl of assorted vegetables (chopped drumsticks, yellow pumpkin, white pumpkin, carrots and potatoes)
½ tomato, chopped
½ onion, chopped
¼ tsp. sambhar masala
1 tsp. oil
A pinch of asafoetida
1 tsp. cumin seeds

Few curry leaves
Salt, as per taste

Directions
- Boil the assorted vegetables.
- In a pressure cooker add 1 spoon of oil or ghee, a pinch of asafoetida, cumin seeds, curry leaves, chopped onion, chopped tomato and sauté.
- Add the toor dal, salt, turmeric and sambhar masala and mix well for 2–3 minutes. Add 1 cup of water and let it whistle 3–4 times. Sambar is ready to be served.

35. Cantonese Egg Fried Rice

Ingredients
2 cups cooked rice
1 tbsp. butter or ghee
1 egg
A pinch of black pepper powder
Salt, as per taste

Directions
- In a bowl, beat the egg.
- Add oil or butter in a frying pan. Add the beaten egg and the cooked rice to it. Sprinkle salt and pepper and mix well. Cook for 1–2 minutes. Serve.

36. Homestyle Toor Dal

Ingredients
1–2 tbsp. toor dal
1 tsp. oil or ghee
1–2 garlic cloves, mashed
A pinch of asafoetida
1 tsp. cumin seeds
¼ tsp. turmeric
Salt, as per taste

Directions
- In a pressure cooker add 1 spoon of oil or ghee, a pinch of asafoetida, cumin seeds, mashed garlic. Add the toor dal, salt and turmeric and mix well for 2–3 minutes.
- Add 1 cup of water and let it whistle 2–3 times. Ready to serve.

Variation: To plain rice, add 2–3 tbsp. of toor dal and ghee. Mash it together and feed your child. In south India, this dish is called Paruppu Sadham.

37. Everyday Masoor Dal

Ingredients
1 tbsp. oil or ghee
1–2 tbsp. masoor dal
1–2 garlic cloves, mashed
A pinch of asafoetida
1 tsp. cumin seeds
¼ tbsp. turmeric
Salt, as per taste

Directions
- In a pressure cooker, add the oil or ghee, a pinch of asafoetida, cumin seeds, mashed garlic.
- Add the masoor dal, salt, turmeric and mix well for 2–3 minutes.
- Add 1 cup of water and let it whistle 2–3 times. Ready to serve.

38. Wonderful Urad Dal

Ingredients
2–3 tbsp. urad dal
2–3 garlic cloves, mashed
1 tbsp. ghee or oil
A pinch of asafoetida
¼ tsp. cumin seeds
Salt, as per taste

Directions
- In a pressure cooker add the oil or ghee, a pinch of asafoetida, cumin seeds, mashed garlic.
- Add the urad dal and salt and mix well for 2–3 minutes.
- Add 1 cup of water and let it whistle 2–3 times. Ready to serve.

REMEDIES

1. Kashyaam (for cold and congestion)

Ingredients
10 gm jaggery
Small piece of ginger
1 tsp. ajwain (carom)

Directions
- In a pan add 1 cup of water, jaggery, ginger and ajwain. Boil for 5–6 minutes.
- Let it cool and serve.

2. Herbal Ginger Honey

Ingredients
Small piece of mashed ginger
1 tsp. honey
A pinch of turmeric powder

Directions
- Squeeze the juice of the mashed ginger and add the honey to the ginger and mix well.

Acknowledgements

I'd like to begin by thanking my Guruji, Shri Amma Bhagwan, for all the blessings and good wishes I have received. My gratitude is boundless.

I want to thank my soul sister, Natasha Jitender Irani. We've known each other all our lives. When I first hesitatingly told her about this book, asking her if she thought I could do something like this, she loved the idea immediately. '*Bitli* (my pet name), just do it!' she commanded. 'I'm so excited for you.' I had not shared the idea with anyone, and she pushed me to explore it. Thank you for that initial push, the encouragement and for giving me the confidence that I, too, could be an author. This book would not have happened had it not been for you.

Thank you, Jaya aunty, for writing the Foreword to the book. She's the epitome of the perfect woman and mother who has brought up both her children—Abhishek and Shweta—beautifully. I've looked up to her all my life and I can't thank her enough for her precious words—they mean the world to me and I will cherish them forever.

A big thank you to the journalist and the man who made my film, *Cakewalk*—Ram Kamal Mukherjee (who also penned my mother's biography). When I told him about my idea, he immediately helped me navigate the world of publishing. I was clueless about authors and publishing houses prior to his guidance. He introduced me to Penguin Random House, and I was fortunate that they loved the idea. Ram knows that Radhya calls me Amma, and when we were talking about the book, he jokingly suggested that I call the book *Amma Mia*! And I loved the way it sounded. Thank you, Ram, for this cute title. More so because today, Radhya calls her little sister Mia (Miraya)!

Thank you, Subi, for the fun book-cover shoot with my two girls! You know I could only trust you with it. Thank you for capturing us so beautifully.

Thanks in abundance to Shivani Rukhana Takhtani and Vaidehi Ruparel of Two Teaspoons Full for their wonderful food styling, and to Rachit Vora for his delectable recipe shots in the book—they've added a whole new charm to the book.

Thank you to my manager, Pamela, for painstakingly finding method in my madness. She helped me put together all my recipes, which were scribbled on post-its, notes, half-torn papers, accumulating in different diaries and books, or even written in Marathi by my cook, when I had dictated them to her. She put everything together, typed out all the recipes so that it came together as a coherent journal. Thank you for your time, energy and patience.

Thank you, Gurveen Chadha and Trisha Bora at Penguin Random House for making this book a reality.

A big thank you to Dr Ravindra Chittal, one of the best doctors in the country, for his precious time and much needed inputs. They will come in handy for all new mothers.

Thank you Dr Suneeta Banerjee—a wonderful woman who treats all her patients with such love and care. I'm privileged to have you be a part of this book.

Now, we come to my angels and my children's guardians. Thank you Bharti, for always being there (from the first chapter in this book!). She's fed and looked after me and my sister and now she does the same for my babies. She's a short, chubby Maharashtrian woman who talks nineteen-to-a-dozen. In every video I've taken of my babies, Bharti's voice is always a fixed presence. In fact, most times, we can hear Bharti before we see her! She also makes the best rasam in the world! Thank you for being you, the most trustworthy and unconditional person I know. I love you and I wish you the best health and happiness and for your children. You are family.

When I was pregnant for the first time and was going to be a first-time mother, I was anxious about being able to find a responsible nurse. I interviewed at least thirty to forty nurses, and when I met Sister Vijaya, I immediately knew she was the one. I didn't even ask her too many questions, I just listened to my gut, and it told me that she was perfect. A Malayali woman in her early fifties, Sister Vijaya is dedicated, extremely energetic and excellent beyond words. And, she looks after both my babies. She was the one who first got Radhya to try something other than milk (remember the bottle gourd soup story? That's her!). She takes a lot of pride in the trust I put in her.

A soft-spoken, loving Christian woman, Valina is Radhya's current nanny. She's extremely hard-working and an excellent cook herself. She joined us when Radhya was transitioning to mashed food, and she immediately put her cooking skills to the test.

Thank you Prabha, our in-house help, who brought in a completely different palate and flavour of food for the babies. She learned quickly and immediately picked up recipes that I'd ideated with her. Thank you for writing down all the recipes in Marathi, especially when I was rambling!

Marrisa came into our home for a very short span, when Radhya was having her liquid soups and we were going to travel abroad. But in that short period, she wowed me with her cooking skills. Thank you for enhancing Radhya's taste palate by making the most delicious mashed food! She was the first person who told me that a baby could have Thai curry, albeit when it's mashed and non-spicy! Before her, I thought mashed food was only potatoes and stewed apples and pears. Thank you for all the help and I wish you all the best.

Now, I'd like to thank my mother-in-law, Puja Takhtani, who showed me how to be an ideal housewife and manage a kitchen, which I'd never seen before. She also encouraged me to cook. I thank her for showing me how to spread love through food.

Thank you Papa (Dharamji), for the love and emotional support. A big thank you to my sister Ahana for all the support through both my pregnancies, and for all the advice and tips. My sister is a fabulous cook; her rosemary pasta is something I can never say no to when I'm at hers. I hope this book comes in handy for your number two!

Finally, I want to thank my mother for just being her—this superwoman in all our lives. I don't have the words to express my gratitude for her, and yet, at the same time, I can write a whole book on how much I love her. You are everything to me. She's made me the woman I am today. I thank you for letting me make my own choices, for letting me make mistakes and for being the best example to learn from. I love you.

Acknowledgements

A big thank you to the most important man in my life, my husband, Bharat, for making me a cook! If it wasn't for you, I wouldn't have transformed that utilitarian kitchen of mine into an actual kitchen, nor would I have started the gas and fried a potato to make it good enough to eat! Thank you for enjoying my food and never getting a stomach ache when eating it! Thank you for encouraging me to pursue my dreams and for egging me on to write this book. And most of all, for our two beautiful babies. None of this would've been possible without you.

I want to thank my two babies, Radhya and Miraya, for making me the best mother I can be. Motherhood has helped me open a new dimension in my life and it truly is a sweet, sweet journey. Motherhood doesn't end things for you; in fact, it's just the opposite. My initial journey as a new mother inspired me to write this book and become an author, adding another feather to my cap. I thank them both for transforming me into Chef Amma Mia! And I hope, in the future, when both of you become mamas and have your own babies, you can look back at this book to guide you on your own journeys.

A Note on the Author

Esha Deol Takhtani is an Indian film actor with hits such as *Dhoom*, *Na Tum Jaano Na Hum*, *Yuva*, *No Entry* and *Dus* to her credit. She recently portrayed the role of a chef in the short film *Cakewalk*, which was released globally on a digital platform and has won a cascade of awards worldwide.

Seeing her illustrious mother, Hema Malini, blazing a trail in classical dance, Esha too succumbed to its lure. She decided to hone her skills in Odissi and in this she was enthusiastically supported by her mother. She has mastered many special renditions in the Odissi repertoire, with over a hundred performances—both solo and in partnership with her younger sister, Ahana. Her depiction of the lovable Sita, the wife of Lord Rama, in the ballet Ramayana has charmed audiences the world over.

Married to a businessman, Bharat Takhtani, Esha is now a doting mother to two daughters—Radhya and Miraya. Esha has recently ventured into production with her first film, which is set to go on floors soon.

New York special avocado purée

Baby Takhtani's famous bottle-gourd soup

Miraya relishing her bottle-gourd soup

Boosting zucchini and asparagus soup

Snacky sooji

Dream Girl's sweet pongal

Continental potato wrap

Surprising mixed vegetable idlis

Egg palak powerhouse

Swadikha Thai curry (for babies aged 6–12 months, purée in a grinder first)

Semolina appam

Baby's sweet tooth gajar ka halwa

Valina's famous bread pudding

Refreshing mango sooji

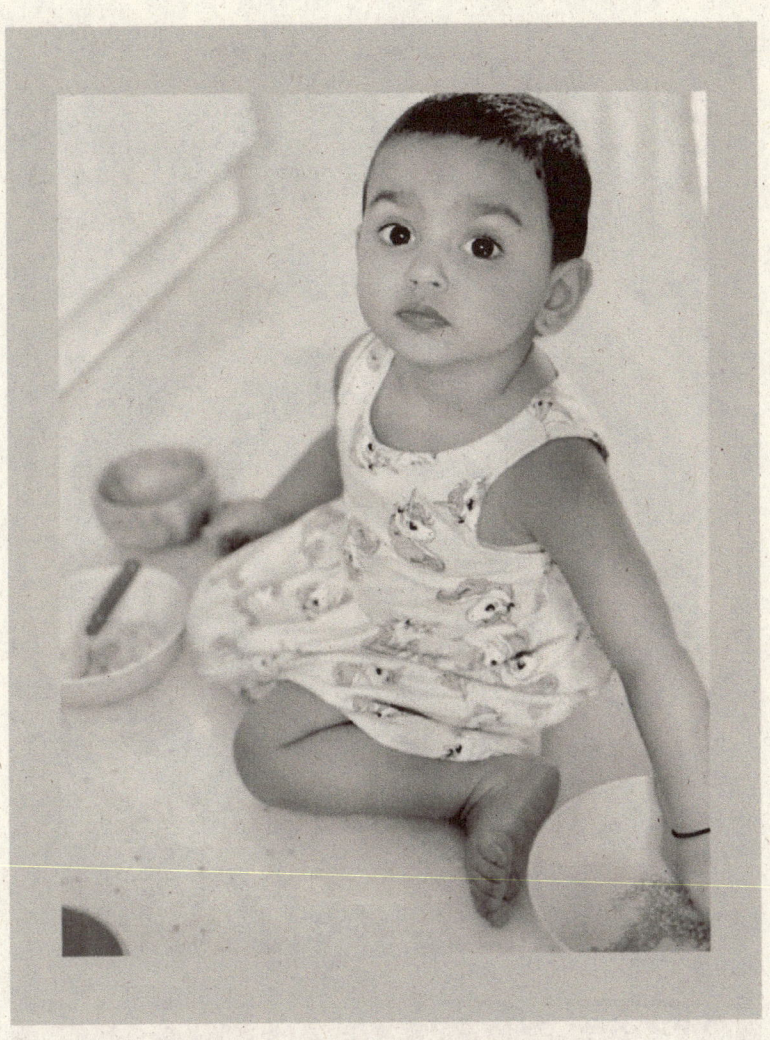

Radhya enjoying the process of food weaning

Soothing baked apple with rice